Pasta & Co.

Pasta & Co.

spaghetti, ravioli, lasagna and more

A Leonardo Publishing Book

summary

A Mediterranean Legend

The exact origins of pasta lie buried in the mists of time, with a number of contenders vying for paternity. What is clear is that pasta's history goes back millennia, and that today pasta is above all a "made in Italy" phenomenon, successfully exported around the world.

A very primitive form of pasta may have been created about 7,000 years ago, when human beings first made the switch from a nomadic lifestyle to agriculture. In many ways the history of pasta begins with the history of wheat, its cultivation and its grinding into flour. We know that in every part of the world there are bread-like foods, whether chapati, tortillas or focaccias, which often ended up cut into strips and immersed in soups and other sauces, almost a kind of prototypical tagliatelle.

Today in Italy there are two broad divisions of pasta. *Pasta fresca*, fresh pasta, is based on a flour-and-egg dough and is not kept for long before use, while *pasta secca* is dried and can be stored for fairly long periods of time.

The legend of Italian homemade pasta, despite being somewhat of a myth, has nonetheless become an expression of the culture and traditions (not just culinary) of individual regions and other geographical areas.

Pasta has played a fundamental role in the cuisine of the Mediterranean since ancient times. The Romans apparently imported the tradition of *lagane*, a kind of thin pasta which was fried or boiled, from the Greeks. While this was a predecessor of our modern lasagne, it was the Arabs who first dried pasta and contributed to its spread throughout Italy.

A ribbon-like pasta made from hard wheat, *trie*, first appeared in Palermo, while macaroni were first documented in Genoa in 1279.

Pasta production in Naples came much later, but it was here that macaroni became a food for popular consumption.

Starting in the eighteenth century, the pasta could be bought from stalls and was eaten by hand on street corners.

a curiosity
Different pasta shapes are not just an aesthetic quirk, but actually have a profound impact on taste. Flavor changes with the pasta's form, which influences its ability to hold sauce.

The classic marriage of pasta and tomatoes came only at the beginning of the 19th century, following widespread acceptance of the New World fruit as a food.

Since then, pasta has been the star of Italian tables around the peninsula.

The Shapes of Taste

More than 300 different kinds of pasta are produced in Italy. They are classified according to the flour used (hard or soft wheat) and their shape.

The shape is the key to the harmonious union of sauce and pasta, and each variation in the endless parade of forms offers a different sensation on the palate.

The classic division of dried pasta is between long and short shapes, with short shapes further subdivided between smooth or ridged.

In general, the longer shapes pair well with thinner, more fluid, fresh tomato sauces with fish or other seafood.

Short pastas are best matched with thicker, heartier sauces, such as meat or vegetable ragùs.

For optimum results, thinner shapes can be drained while still undercooked, then finished in the pan with the sauce.

This process allows the sauce to soak into the center of the pasta, resulting in a fuller and more intense flavor.

How to Recognize Good Pasta

Pasta is made from just a few, simple ingredients, so many other secondary elements in its preparation take on great importance.

The techniques of preparation, cooking and sauce-making are all subject to hints, tips, secrets and kitchen lore.

Some of these may be based solely on popular belief, but more often they arise from good sense and astuteness which has evolved over time and been

advice

When making fresh pasta, create a rougher surface by rolling the dough out with a rolling pin rather than a pasta machine. Remember to remove any excess flour clinging to the pasta before cooking it in boiling water.

Pasta

passed down through the generations. Once again it is worth noting the obvious, that cuisine is not just about food and nutrition, but also culture.

It is now possible to buy many different kinds of fresh pasta, in both supermarkets and specialty stores, but quite apart from the factors concerning taste, there is a whole series of cultural elements, linked to the "human" side of gastronomy, which cannot be ignored.

Skill, care, experience and the right ingredients are what go into making an exceptional fresh pasta.

The raw materials count for 60%, dough mixing for 30% and technology for 10% in terms of the quality of the final product.

The flour for pasta is ground from a mix of grains, with the best coming from Puglia in Italy, Arizona in the U.S., and Canada.

Puglian grain has a good ability to maintain consistency during cooking. However, it has a pale color and is low in protein, so it is usually mixed with Arizona grain.

Here are some guidelines on how to recognize good-quality pasta.

Cooking Water

The foam that rises to the surface when pasta is added to boiling water is not a sign of bad quality; rather, this effect is simply caused by air bubbles. However, the best pastas generally produce less foam.

When pasta is drained, the water should still be clear. If cloudy, some of the pasta's starch has dissolved, meaning that a grain blend of poor quality was used for the flour.

Cooking Secrets

The key to making a good pasta dish is not just in buying high-quality pasta made with the best ingredients and techniques, but also in following some simple rules of cooking:

color

Dried pasta should have a luminous, uniform aspect, without any cracks or stains. The color should be amber-yellow, but never too dark. An overly "toasted" color can indicate the presence of soft wheat, and above all is a sign that the pasta was dried at overly high temperatures, probably to save time.

■ Use at least 4 cups (1 l) of water for every 3^1/$_2$ oz (100 g) of pasta. Use a large, high-sided pot so that the temperature of the water remains constant. This prevents the pasta from sticking together.

■ Once the water reaches a full boil (never before), add about 1 teaspoon of sea salt for every 3^1/$_2$ oz (100 g) of pasta, and let the salt dissolve.

■ Only add the pasta when the water has returned to a full boil. Because adding the pasta leads to a decrease in water temperature, it is advisable to raise the heat at this point in order to maintain a full boil.

■ Long pasta should be spread out like a fan and never broken, while short pasta should be sprinkled in to avoid clumping together at the bottom of the pot. Pasta nests should be immersed in water and then immediately unraveled with the help of a large fork or a wooden spoon.

■ Gently stir the pasta frequently at the beginning to stop it from sticking, and then every so often during the rest of the cooking time.

■ Drain the pasta when it is al dente ("to the tooth"), meaning it gives just a little resistance when bitten into. While every pasta shape has its own cooking time, the best way to see if it is done. A sample piece of pasta can also be broken: If it is still white in the center, then it needs to cook for about another minute.

■ When it's ready, drain the pasta, reserving a little of the cooking water in case the sauce needs to be thinned.

■ Transfer the drained pasta to a serving bowl and quickly toss with the sauce so that it is uniformly absorbed. If the recipe calls for the cooked pasta to be sautéed in a pan, drain it a minute before it is done and finish cooking in the sauce, over high heat.

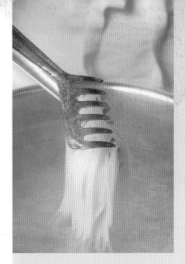

the basic rules

Do not rinse the pasta under cold water because it will lose the layer of starch that helps the sauce adhere.

The only exceptions are when making cold pasta dishes, or with some particularly buttery sauces.

Pasta

9

contents

dried pasta

Pasta

paccheri with radicchio and sausage

Ingredients for 4 servings

Paccheri:

1/2 tsp fennel seeds

3 tbsps extra-virgin olive oil

1 small yellow onion, minced

5½ oz (150 g) sausage

1 garlic clove, unpeeled and smashed

1 head of radicchio, preferably Treviso

2 tbsps milk

salt and pepper

14 oz (400 g) paccheri or anelli pasta

9 oz (250 g) primosale cheese, or other soft, mild cheese, diced

Grind the fennel seeds with a mortar and pestle.
Heat the olive oil in a frying pan and gently sauté
the onion. Add the fennel seeds.
Meanwhile trim the white stalks of the radicchio leaves,
and finely slice the red parts.
Remove the skin from the sausage and crumble the meat
into the frying pan with the onions.
Add the garlic. Brown the meat for 1 minute, then add
the radicchio. Sauté for 5 minutes then add the milk
and adjust salt and pepper.
Bring a large pot of salted water to a boil and cook
the paccheri. Drain and add to the sauce together with the
cheese. Stir well, then serve immediately.

This pasta can also be gratinéed in
the oven after being topped with
a little grated Parmesan cheese
or some béchamel sauce.

Preparation time **15 minutes**
Cooking time **20 minutes**
Level **easy**
Wine **Nero d'Avola**

pasta wheels with fennel carbonara

Ingredients for 4 servings
Wheels:

1 large fennel bulb, cut into wedges

salt and pepper

2 tbsps extra-virgin olive oil

4 oz (120 g) guanciale, julienned

1 garlic clove, thickly sliced

2 eggs

1 tbsp grated Pecorino Romano cheese

2 tbsps grated Parmesan cheese

1 tbsp heavy cream

14 oz (400 g) pasta wheels (ruote)

Steam the fennel wedges or boil them in lightly salted water until tender. Drain and chop.
Heat the olive oil in a non-stick frying pan and sauté the guanciale and garlic.
Beat the eggs with the grated Pecorino, grated Parmesan, salt and pepper. Stir in the cream.
Bring a large pot of salted water to a boil and cook the pasta.
Meanwhile remove the garlic from the frying pan and add the fennel. Sauté until lightly browned.
Drain the pasta when al dente and add to the pan with the fennel and guanciale.
Stir well then remove from the heat.
Pour the egg mixture over the pasta and mix thoroughly. The sauce should be creamy but the eggs should not scramble. Serve immediately.

Guanciale looks similar to pancetta, with white fat streaked with leaner veins of meat, but it is made from a cut of the pig's cheek and neck, while pancetta comes from the belly.

Preparation time **15 minutes**
Cooking time **25 minutes**
Level **easy**
Wine **Colli del Trasimeno Bianco**

anelli with eggplant and tomato

Ingredients for 4 servings
Anelli:

1 small, long eggplant, cut lengthwise into wedges

salt and pepper

3 tbsps extra-virgin olive oil

1 shallot, minced

1/2 red chili pepper, deseeded and minced

thyme leaves

15 cherry tomatoes, quartered and deseeded

14 oz (400 g) anelli or paccheri pasta

1 cow's milk mozzarella (about 7 oz or 200 g), diced

Salt the eggplant wedges and leave to drain in a colander for at least 30 minutes.
Drain the eggplant and remove the central, seedy part. Dice the rest.
Heat the olive oil and sauté the shallot with the chili until soft. Add the eggplant and sauté over high heat for 5 minutes. Add the thyme leaves and tomatoes.
Season lightly with salt and pepper and cook for another 5 minutes.
Meanwhile bring a large pot of salted water to a boil and cook the pasta until al dente.
Drain and add to the pan with the eggplant and tomatoes, together with a little of the pasta cooking water if necessary to thin the sauce.
Toss to coat then stir in the mozzarella.

Add extra color and flavor to this dish by stirring in a tablespoon of basil pesto just before serving.

Preparation time **15 minutes**
Cooking time **10 minutes**
Level **easy**
Wine **Sicilia Chardonnay**

gnocchi with speck, peas and feta

Ingredients for 4 servings
Gnocchi:

3 tbsps extra-virgin olive oil

1 shallot, minced

1⅓ cups (6 oz or 170 g) peas

1 thick slice of speck (around 1 oz
or 30 g), diced

salt and black pepper

12½ oz (350 g) dried hard-wheat
gnocchi pasta

2 oz (60 g) feta cheese, crumbled

Heat the olive oil and sauté the shallot with a little water.
Add the peas and cook for 4 minutes over low heat.
Add the speck and 1 ladleful of hot water.
Cook for another 2-3 minutes.
Bring a large pot of salted water to a boil and cook
the gnocchi until al dente.
Drain and add to the pan with the peas and speck.
Let them absorb the liquid from the sauce, then sprinkle
over the feta.
Finish with a sprinkling of black pepper and serve.

The feta can be replaced by
2 tablespoons fresh ricotta,
mixed with a little of the liquid
from the sauce then added to
the sauce with the pasta. This
makes for a creamier sauce.

Preparation time **10 minutes**
Cooking time **20 minutes**
Level **easy**
Wine **Tocai Friulano**

bucatini with bacon and pecorino

Ingredients for 4 servings
Bucatini:

3½ tbsps (2 oz or 50 g) butter

1 onion, finely minced

4 oz (120 g) bacon, cut into matchsticks

salt and pepper

12½ oz (350 g) bucatini

3 tbsps grated Pecorino
Romano cheese

3 tbsps grated Parmesan cheese

parsley, minced

Melt the butter in a large frying pan and sauté the onion.
Add the bacon and brown for a few minutes.
Bring a large pot of salted water to a boil and cook
the bucatini until al dente.
Drain, reserving the cooking water, and toss in the pan
with the onion and bacon.
Add a little of the reserved cooking water to form a sauce.
Sprinkle over the Pecorino Romano and Parmesan.
Serve hot, finished with freshly ground black pepper
and some minced parsley.

This is a simplified version,
minus the tomatoes, of the
famous bucatini all'amatriciana.

Preparation time **5 minutes**
Cooking time **8 minutes**
Level **easy**
Wine **Cerveteri Rosso**

torchietti with radicchio, artichokes and speck

Ingredients for 4 servings
Torchietti:

2 small artichokes, salt and pepper

14 oz (400 g) dried egg torchietti or fusilli pasta

4 tbsps extra-virgin olive oil

2 garlic cloves, unpeeled and halved

2½ oz (70 g) speck, cut into matchsticks

1 radicchio, preferably Treviso, thinly sliced

parsley, minced

3 tbsps aged ricotta shavings

Trim the artichokes, cutting off the tips and the stems and removing the hard external leaves. Remove the choke. Slice the artichokes thinly, then set aside.

Bring a large pot of salted water to a boil, then add the pasta and cook until al dente.

Meanwhile heat the olive oil and sauté the garlic until golden. Add the speck and sauté, then add the artichokes and sauté over high heat.

Add the radicchio and season with salt and pepper.

Add a little of the pasta cooking water and sprinkle with minced parsley.

Drain the pasta and add to the pan with the sauce. Sauté briefly, reducing the sauce, then serve topped with the ricotta shavings.

Artichokes have a high iron content and can leave a metallic taste in the mouth, making it hard to pair them with wine. Rice and pasta dishes can go well with a light rosé, while fried artichokes and frittatas are best with a structured, soft white.

Preparation time **10 minutes**
Cooking time **15 minutes**
Level **easy**
Wine **Val d'Aosta Pinot Nero**

caserecce with clams and zucchini

Ingredients for 4 servings
Caserecce:

1 lb (500 g) clams

3 tbsps extra-virgin olive oil

1 garlic clove, minced

1/2 dried red chili pepper, crumbled

1 zucchini, deseeded and diced

10 cherry tomatoes, quartered

parsley, minced, salt

14 oz (400 g) caserecce, campanelle
or fusilli pasta

Wash the clams well under cold running water, scrubbing them with a stiff brush.
Let them soak in cold salted water for at least an hour.
Heat the olive oil in a frying pan and sauté the garlic with the chili. Add the zucchini and brown for 1 minute, then add the clams.
Cover and cook over high heat until the clams open, adding the tomatoes after a couple of minutes.
Sprinkle with parsley.
Shell the clams and return them to the sauce.
Bring a large pot of salted water to a boil and cook the pasta until still very al dente.
Drain and add directly to the clams.
Sauté in the pan to reduce the sauce. Serve hot.

This recipe works with any variety of small clams; choose the freshest possible.

Preparation time **20 minutes**
Cooking time **15 minutes**
Level **medium**
Wine **Roero Arneis**

campanelle with peppers and escarole

Ingredients for 4 servings
Campanelle:

1/2 head escarole, shredded

3 tbsps extra-virgin olive oil

1 garlic clove, smashed

12 black Gaeta olives

1/2 red bell pepper, finely diced

thyme, minced

salt and pepper

14 oz (400 g) dried egg campanelle, gigli or garganelli pasta

grated Pecorino Romano

or aged ricotta salata

Soak the escarole in a bowl of cold water.
Heat 2 tablespoons olive oil and sauté the garlic until golden. Drain the escarole and add to the pan.
Stir well, season with salt and cook, covered, for 5 minutes. Add the olives and a little water, cover again, and cook until the escarole is tender and transparent.
Heat 1 tablespoon olive oil in a frying pan and sauté the bell pepper with the thyme until soft.
Bring a large pot of salted water to a boil and cook the pasta until al dente.
Drain and add to the pan with the bell pepper.
Add the escarole and season to taste with pepper.
Stir well. Serve the pasta with grated Pecorino Romano or aged ricotta salata.

The color of olives does not come from the variety, but from ripeness. Underripe olives are green, and later reach a deep black-violet color when fully ripe. One of the best-known olive varieties is Gaeta, with a lightly bitter flavor and a gentle acidity.

Preparation time **15 minutes**
Cooking time **20 minutes**
Level **easy**
Wine **Falerno Bianco**

pasta shells with porcini mushrooms and squash blossoms

Ingredients for 4 servings

Pasta Shells:

3 tbsps extra-virgin olive oil

2 shallots, minced

1 large fresh porcini mushroom (about 5½ oz or 150 g), chopped

1⅓ cups (3½ oz or 100 g) chopped white mushrooms

salt and pepper

8 squash blossoms, finely chopped

1/2 cup (120 ml) vegetable broth

1 tbsp heavy cream, **1** tsp cornstarch

11 oz (300 g) large pasta shells

parsley, minced

To preserve mushrooms' fragrance, they should not be washed or peeled, just wiped clean with a damp paper towel and then dried. If they are particularly dirty they can be washed under running water, but never soak them.

Heat 2 tablespoons olive oil in a frying pan and add 1 shallot. Sauté over low heat and then add the mushrooms. Season with salt and pepper and sauté for 10 minutes.

Meanwhile, heat the remaining olive oil in a small saucepan and add the remaining shallot.

When the shallot is soft, add the squash blossoms. Pour over the broth and cook for 5 minutes.

Add the cream and whisk in the cornstarch to thicken the sauce.

Bring a large pot of salted water to a boil and cook the pasta shells until al dente.

Drain and fill with the mushrooms.

Sprinkle with parsley and serve on top of the squash blossom sauce.

Preparation time **20 minutes**
Cooking time **30 minutes**
Level **easy**
Wine **Trentino Müller Thurgau**

rice spaghetti with seitan and peas

Ingredients for 4 servings
Rice Spaghetti:

4 tbsps extra-virgin olive oil

1 spring onion, thinly sliced

salt

1 cup (5½ oz or 150 g) shelled peas

2/3 cup (3½ oz or 100 g) cherry tomatoes

7 oz (200 g) seitan, cut into strips

8½ oz (240 g) rice spaghetti

1 tbsp minced parsley

Heat a drizzle of olive oil in a frying pan and sauté the spring onion with a pinch of salt.
Add the peas and a little water, cover and cook for 10 minutes. Add the cherry tomatoes and seitan.
Season with salt and cook for another 5 minutes.
Bring a large pot of salted water to the boil and cook the spaghetti. Drain, immerse in cold water, drain again then transfer to the frying pan with the sauce.
Drizzle with the remaining olive oil, sprinkle with parsley and mix well before serving.

Seitan is a wheat gluten with a high protein content, low in fat and cholesterol-free. However it is low in iron and so should not be considered a meat substitute, unlike soy derivatives.

Preparation time **10 minutes**
Cooking time **20 minutes**
Level **easy**
Wine **Friuli Collio Tocai**

spinach, mushroom and salmon fusilli

Ingredients for 4 servings
Fusilli:

3 tbsps extra-virgin olive oil

2⅔ cups (7 oz or 200 g) sliced mushrooms

salt and pepper

7 oz (200 g) salmon fillet, diced

10½ oz (300 g) spinach, chopped

2 tbsps heavy cream

12½ oz (350 g) fusilli

Heat the olive oil in a large frying pan, add the mushrooms and sauté for 3-4 minutes.
Season with salt, add the salmon and spinach and cook for a couple of minutes. Add the cream and remove from heat. Bring a large pot of salted water to a boil and cook the fusilli until al dente.
Drain and toss with the sauce. Return to the heat and cook for 2 minutes. Sprinkle with pepper and serve hot.

Fusilli originated in the center of Italy, and their name comes from the fuso, the spindle around which yarn is wrapped. Their spiral form makes them perfect for holding sauce.

Preparation time **20 minutes**
Cooking time **10 minutes**
Level **easy**
Wine **Bianco dei Castelli Romani**

corn fusilli with green beans and squash

Ingredients for 4 servings

Corn Fusilli:

3 tbsps extra-virgin olive oil

1/2 shallot, minced

1 garlic clove, halved

1/4 leek, finely sliced

1/2 dried red chili pepper, deseeded

2 cups (9 oz or 250 g) diced summer squash

salt and pepper

2 cups (7 oz or 200 g) green beans

1/2 cup (120 ml) hot vegetable broth

1 tomato, **14** oz (400 g) corn fusilli

Heat the olive oil and sauté the shallot, garlic and leek. Crumble in the chili pepper.
As soon as the shallot is transparent remove the garlic and add the summer squash.
Season with salt and pepper and continue cooking. Meanwhile top and tail the green beans, blanch for 3 minutes in salted water and immerse immediately in ice water. Cut into bite-sized pieces, add to the squash together with a little hot broth and continue cooking. Remove the seeds from the tomato and cut the flesh into strips. Add to the pan and season with salt and pepper. Bring a large pot of salted water to a boil and cook the fusilli until still very al dente.
Drain and toss with the vegetables and broth until cooked through.

Green beans, also known as French beans or haricots verts, are bean pods which are young and tender enough to be eaten whole. They can be stored in the refrigerator, closed in a plastic bag, for 3-4 days.

Preparation time **20 minutes**
Cooking time **20 minutes**
Level **easy**
Wine **Colli di Luni Bianco**

spicy sardinian gnocchetti
with cuttlefish and peas

Ingredients for 4 servings
Gnocchetti:

2 small cuttlefish with ink sacs

2 tbsps extra-virgin olive oil

1 shallot, minced

1 red chili pepper, minced

15 fresh pea pods

3/4 cup (180 ml) fish broth

salt and pepper

13½ oz (380 g) Sardinian gnocchetti, gemelli or fusilli pasta

thyme and parsley, minced

1 tomato, diced (optional)

Clean the cuttlefish, removing the guts, eye and central bone. Detach the ink sacs and set aside carefully. Rinse the cuttlefish. Heat the olive oil and sauté the shallot with the chili until soft.
Shell the peas and add them to the sautéed shallot. Cook, covered, adding a little broth from time to time. Cut the cuttlefish into strips and add to the peas after 5 minutes. Continue cooking until the cuttlefish is cooked through and the peas are tender.
Mix the cuttlefish ink with a little broth and then add it to the sauce. Season with salt and pepper to taste. Bring a large pot of salted water to a boil and cook the pasta until al dente. Drain and add to the sauce together with the thyme and parsley. Mix well.
Use a round cookie cutter to plate the pasta on serving dishes and serve immediately, garnished with diced tomatoes if desired.

The chili has a number of virtues, being high in vitamin C, as well as vitamins A, E, K and P.P. It helps prevent cardiovascular disease as well as facilitating wound healing.

Preparation time **15 minutes**
Cooking time **20 minutes**
Level **easy**
Wine **Vermentino di Sardegna**

lasagnetta with potatoes, porcini and thyme

Ingredients for 4 servings
Lasagnetta:

4 tbsps extra-virgin olive oil

1 shallot, minced

2 large yellow-fleshed potatoes, peeled and diced

rosemary, chopped

salt and pepper

1/2 cup (120 ml) mushroom or vegetable broth

3 fresh porcini mushrooms, cleaned and diced

thyme leaves

14 oz (400 g) lasagnette

Heat the olive oil in a frying pan.
Add the shallot and sauté until soft.
Add the potatoes, rosemary and salt and pepper to taste.
Add the mushroom or vegetable broth, and cook
for 7-8 minutes. Add the porcini mushrooms and thyme.
Bring a large pot of salted water to a boil.
Boil the lasagna sheets, then drain.
Toss with the sauce and serve immediately.

For extra color, use 8 regular lasagna sheets and 8 spinach lasagna sheets, then compose the serving plates by alternating the different colors with spoonfuls of sauce.

Preparation time **10 minutes**
Cooking time **20 minutes**
Level **easy**
Wine **Lagrein Rosato**

farro linguine with vegetable ragù and geranium flowers

Ingredients for 4 servings

Linguine:

2 tbsps corn oil

1 small onion, diced

1 carrot, diced

1/2 red bell pepper, diced

salt and pepper

1 small eggplant, diced

2 zucchini, diced

1 tsp tomato paste

1/2 cup (120 ml) water

10½ oz (300 g) farro linguine

red geranium flowers

Heat the corn oil in a frying pan and sauté the onion.
Add the carrot and bell pepper, season with salt and cook over high heat for 5 minutes.
Add the eggplant and zucchini and sauté for a few minutes.
Dissolve the tomato concentrate in the water and add to the vegetables.
Cover and cook over low heat for 15 minutes.
Meanwhile bring a large pot of salted water to a boil and cook the linguine until al dente.
Drain, reserving some of the cooking water, and transfer to the frying pan with the vegetables.
Add the geranium flowers, salt and pepper and sauté for 1 minute, until thoroughly combined.
Add the reserved cooking water if the sauce is too dry.
Serve hot, sprinkled with geranium flowers.

Preparation time **20 minutes**
Cooking time **35 minutes**
Level **easy**
Wine **Bolgheri Bianco**

rigatoni with chickpeas and seaweed

Ingredients for 4 servings

Rigatoni:

1/2 cup (3½ oz or 100 g) dried chickpeas, soaked overnight

2 bay leaves

2 tbsps hijiki seaweed

extra-virgin olive oil

1 garlic clove

soy sauce

12 oz (350 g) whole-wheat rigatoni

salt

Boil the chickpeas with 2 bay leaves in a pressure cooker for 50 minutes.
Soak the seaweed in cold water for 10 minutes, then drain and chop.
Heat the olive oil in a frying pan and add the garlic.
Let brown and then add the seaweed.
Add the chickpeas and soy sauce to taste and sauté briefly.
Bring a pot of salted water to a boil and cook the rigatoni until al dente.
Drain and transfer to the pan with the sauce.
Sauté for 1 minute and serve immediately.

Preparation time **15 minutes**
Cooking time **1 hour 15 minutes**
Level **easy**
Wine **Lugana**

fried spaghetti
with wild mushroom ragù

Ingredients for 4 servings
Spaghetti:

10 cherry tomatoes

3 garlic cloves

4 tbsps extra-virgin olive oil

salt and pepper

10½ oz (300 g) thin spaghetti

3/4 cup (3½ oz or 100 g) diced onion

3/4 cup (3½ oz or 100 g) diced celery

3/4 cup (3½ oz or 100 g) diced carrot

1 dried red chili pepper

3 cups (10½ oz or 300 g) mixed wild mushrooms, (porcini, chanterelles, honey mushrooms), cleaned and chopped

1/2 cup (3 oz or 80 g) crushed tomatoes

1 tsp tomato concentrate

parsley, chopped

Preheat the oven to 325°F (170°C or Gas Mark 3). Place the cherry tomatoes on a baking sheet with the garlic cloves and 1 tablespoon olive oil. Roast for 30 minutes. Line a rectangular baking dish with parchment paper. Bring a large pot of salted water to a boil and cook the spaghetti until still very al dente. Drain and place pasta in the baking dish.
Cover the pasta with a sheet of parchment paper and place another baking dish on top of the pasta. Heat 2 tablespoons olive oil in a large frying pan. Add the onion, celery, carrot and chili pepper. Sauté briefly. Add the mushrooms and sauté for another 7-8 minutes. Remove from the heat and drain any excess liquid. Dice the mixture. Place in a saucepan with the crushed tomatoes, tomato concentrate, parsley and salt and pepper to taste. Cook over low heat until thickened. Remove the pasta block from the baking dish and slice. Heat the remaining olive oil in a large frying pan and fry the pasta slices. Top the fried pasta slices with ragù and roasted cherry tomatoes and serve immediately.

Preparation time **20 minutes**
Cooking time **1 hour**
Level **easy**
Wine **Blanc de Morgex et de La Salle**

sedanini with baby squid and tomatoes

Ingredients for 4 servings

Sedanini:

salt and pepper

10½ oz (300 g) durum-wheat ridged sedanini or penne pasta

3 tbsps extra-virgin olive oil

2 ripe tomatoes

parsley, minced

7 oz (200 g) baby squid

1/2 garlic clove, finely minced

Bring a large pot of very salty water to the boil and cook the pasta for just 4-5 minutes.
Drain and cool under cold running water.
Toss with a little olive oil and set aside.
Blanch the tomatoes and immerse in cold water.
Peel, deseed and dice. Season with salt and pepper and sprinkle over the parsley.
Steam the baby squid for 2 minutes, mix with a little minced garlic and stir into the pasta with the tomatoes.
Mix well and serve.

Preparation time **20 minutes**
Cooking time **7 minutes**
Level **easy**
Wine **Castel del Monte Rosato**

penne with shrimp, tomatoes and peas

Ingredients for 4 servings

Penne:

2 tbsps extra-virgin olive oil

1/2 onion, finely minced

1½ cups (7 oz or 200 g) peas

1/2 cup (120 ml) vegetable broth

2 ripe tomatoes

1 garlic clove, halved

10½ oz (300 g) shelled and deveined shrimp

salt and pepper

12½ oz (360 g) ridged penne

parsley, minced

Heat the olive oil in a frying pan and sauté the onion. Add the peas and cook for about 10 minutes, gradually adding the vegetable broth.
Blanch the tomato in boiling water for 30 seconds, then drain, peel, deseed and chop.
Add to the onion and peas together with the garlic.
Cook briefly, then add the shrimp.
Adjust salt and pepper and cook for 5 minutes.
Meanwhile bring a large pot of salted water to a boil and cook the penne until al dente.
Drain and toss in the pan with the sauce. Sprinkle with parsley and serve.

Enrich this dish with 1 large zucchini, thinly sliced and added to the frying pan with the peas.

Preparation time **10 minutes**
Cooking time **15 minutes**
Level **easy**
Wine **Bolgheri Bianco**

mezze maniche with ricotta and basil

Ingredients for 4 servings
Mezze Maniche:

1 garlic clove, halved

3 tbsps extra-virgin olive oil

1 cup (1 oz or 30 g) torn basil leaves

9 oz (250 g) ricotta

salt and pepper

12½ oz (350 g) mezze maniche
or other short pasta

1/4 cup (1 oz or 30 g) sliced
almonds, toasted

Rub the inside of a bowl with the garlic halves.
Place the ricotta in the bowl, add the olive oil, basil
and salt and pepper to taste and mix well.
Bring a large pot of salted water to a boil and cook
the pasta until al dente.
Drain, reserving some cooking water, and transfer
to the bowl with the ricotta mixture. Add a little cooking
water and mix well.
Serve topped with the sliced almonds.

Alternatively, leave out the almonds
and stir in some olive puree
(tapenade) into the ricotta mixture.
Garnish with some minced chives.

Preparation time **5 minutes**
Cooking time **10 minutes**
Level **easy**
Wine **Alto Adige Pinot Bianco**

neapolitan-style pasta and potatoes

Ingredients for 4 servings

Pasta:

1 garlic clove

3 tbsps extra-virgin olive oil

2 oz (60 g) ham, diced

2 medium yellow-fleshed potatoes, peeled and diced

14 oz (400 g) mixed pasta (spaghetti, penne, ziti, fusilli), broken into similar-sized pieces

6 cups (1½ l) vegetable broth or water

salt and pepper

3 tbsps grated Parmesan cheese

1 tbsp grated Pecorino Romano cheese

1 red chili pepper, minced (optional)

Halve the unpeeled garlic clove and remove the green shoot. Heat the olive oil in a large saucepan and sauté the garlic. Add the ham and then the potatoes.
Cook for 2 minutes, stirring frequently.
Cover with a few ladlefuls of vegetable broth or water, then add the pasta.
Continue cooking as though it was a risotto, adding broth or water whenever the liquid has almost evaporated.
Season with salt and pepper, and as soon as the pasta in al dente add a little extra broth and the grated cheeses.
Stir, then remove from the heat.
Cover and let sit for 5 minutes.
Serve hot, garnished with minced chili pepper if desired.

Preparation time **20 minutes**
Cooking time **15 minutes**
Level **easy**
Wine **Fiano di Avellino**

egg riccioli with artichoke and eggplant

Ingredients for 4 servings
Riccioli:

1/2 eggplant, deseeded and cut into strips

3 small artichokes, juice of 1 lemon

4 tbsps extra-virgin olive oil

2 garlic cloves, smashed

1 small leek, thinly sliced

1 dried red chili pepper

1/2 cup (120 ml) hot vegetable broth

1 tomato, diced or cut into thin wedges

salt, parsley, minced

14 oz (400 g) dried egg riccioli or fusilli pasta

Round eggplants are good for cooking sliced, while the longer eggplants are good for dicing or stuffing.

Place the eggplant in a colander and sprinkle with salt. Let sit at least 30 minutes to drain.
Meanwhile, trim the artichokes by cutting off the stem, removing the hard outer leaves and cutting off the leaf tips. Cut in half and scoop out the choke.
Thinly slice the artichokes then let them soak in a bowl of cold water with lemon juice.
Heat the olive oil in a frying pan with the garlic cloves, leek and chili. Let cook over low heat for 5 minutes.
Drain and dry the eggplant and add to the frying pan.
Drain the artichokes and add to the pan as well.
Cook for 6-7 minutes, adding a little hot broth and stirring frequently. Add the tomato, adjust the salt and sprinkle with parsley.
Bring a large pot of salted water to a boil and cook the pasta until al dente.
Drain and add to the pan with the sauce and toss to coat. Serve hot.

Preparation time **15 minutes**
Cooking time **15 minutes**
Level **easy**
Wine **Cinque Terre**

penne with zucchini and pesto

Ingredients for 4 servings

Penne:

1 tbsp extra-virgin olive oil

1 onion, thinly sliced

2 zucchini, sliced, salt

6 squash blossoms, julienned

7 oz (200 g) penne

Pesto:

1 bunch of basil, destemmed

2 tbsps pine nuts, **1/2** tsp barley miso

3 tbsps extra-virgin olive oil

Heat 1 tablespoon olive oil in a frying pan.
Add the onion and 2 tablespoons of water and cook
until soft. Add the zucchini, season with salt and cook
for 10-15 minutes.
Add the squash blossoms and remove from heat.
Make the pesto: Blend the basil, pine nuts, miso and olive
oil in a food processor or with a mortar and pestle.
Bring a large pot of salted water to a boil and cook
the pasta until al dente.
Drain, reserving 2 tablespoons of cooking water, and add
the pasta to the zucchini mixture with the cooking water.
Sauté for a few minutes.
Add the pesto and toss to coat. Serve immediately.

Miso is a brown paste produced from
the fermentation of yellow soy beans, sea
salt and Aspergillus orizae. Sometimes
other ingredients are added, such
as barley, rice or a mixture of both.

Preparation time **20 minutes**
Cooking time **20 minutes**
Level **easy**
Wine **Cinque Terre**

spaghetti with walnut sauce

Ingredients for 6 servings
Spaghetti:

2½ tbsps pine nuts

12 walnuts, shelled

6 tbsps extra-virgin olive oil

1 garlic clove, minced

2 tbsps minced parsley

salt and pepper

1⅓ lb (600 g) spaghetti

grated Parmesan cheese (optional)

Grind the walnuts and pine nuts with a mortar and pestle.
Heat the olive oil in a terracotta casserole or a frying
pan and sauté the garlic and parsley.
Add the walnuts and pine nuts and adjust salt and pepper,
and cook over a low heat for about 10 minutes, stirring
frequently.
Meanwhile bring a large pot of salted water to a boil
and cook the spaghetti until al dente.
Drain and toss with the walnut sauce.
Serve sprinkled with grated Parmesan if desired.

To make a creamier sauce, add
3½ oz (100 g) ricotta, thinned with
a little of the pasta cooking water
to the spaghetti and walnut sauce.

Preparation time **5 minutes**
Cooking time **10 minutes**
Level **easy**
Wine **Falerio dei Colli Ascolani**

paccheri with three peppers in white sauce

Ingredients for 4 servings

Filling:

3 tbsps extra-virgin olive oil

1 garlic clove, smashed

1/2 yellow bell pepper, finely diced

1/2 red bell pepper, finely diced

1/2 green bell pepper, finely diced

9 oz (250 g) sheep's milk ricotta

6 sun-dried tomatoes, 3 minced and 3 julienned

3 tbsps grated Pecorino Romano cheese

salt and pepper, chives, blanched

Sauce:

1 cup (250 ml) milk, **3** garlic cloves

2 tbsps butter, **2½** tbsps cornstarch

hot vegetable broth

Paccheri:

salt, **24** paccheri

Garnish:

3 tbsps extra-virgin olive oil

1 leek, julienned

Preheat the oven to 400°F (200°C or Gas Mark 6).
Heat a little olive oil in a frying pan with the smashed garlic. Sauté one color of pepper at a time, then set aside, keeping the colors separate. Bring the milk to a boil with the 3 garlic cloves and keep warm.
Melt the butter and whisk in the cornstarch, then add the hot milk, discarding the garlic. Whisk until thickened, then whisk in enough hot broth to make a fluid sauce.
Bring a large pot of salted water to a boil.
Cook the paccheri until al dente, drain and cool.
Meanwhile beat the ricotta with the minced sun-dried tomatoes, Pecorino and remaining olive oil.
Season with salt and pepper.
Stuff the cooled paccheri with the ricotta mixture and place them upright on a baking sheet in groups of 6. Tie each cluster with blanched chives and top with sautéed pepper. Bake for 12 minutes.
Heat 3 tablespoons olive oil and fry the julienned leek until golden. Serve the paccheri on the white sauce, topped with the julienned sun-dried tomatoes and fried leek.

Preparation time **25 minutes**
Cooking time **35 minutes**
Level **medium**
Wine **Trentino Nosiola**

spicy greek-style penne

Ingredients for 4 servings

Penne:

7-8 cherry tomatoes, quartered

3 tbsps extra-virgin olive oil

salt

dried hot red chili pepper

oregano

7 oz (200 g) feta cheese, thinly sliced

3/4 cup (3½ oz or 100 g) black olives, pitted

basil, chopped

10½ oz (300 g) ridged penne

Toss the tomatoes with the olive oil, a pinch of salt, some crumbled chili pepper and a pinch of oregano.
Let sit to marinate.
Mix the feta with the olives and basil.
Bring a large pot of salted water to a boil and cook the penne until al dente.
Drain and mix with all the ingredients.
Serve hot or cold.

Chili is such a popular ingredient that some connoisseurs have even founded the Accademia del Peproncino, the Chili Academy, to spread "spicy culture" in Italy.

Preparation time **10 minutes**
Cooking time **10 minutes**
Level **easy**
Wine **Sicilia Chardonnay**

tuscan pici with bread and pecorino

Ingredients for 4 servings

Pici:

7 oz (200 g) stale Tuscan-style bread

1/2 cup (120 ml) extra-virgin olive oil

2 garlic cloves, finely minced, salt

1⅓ lb (600 g) pici or other thick, long pasta (thick spaghetti, bucatini)

5 tbsps grated pecorino cheese

parsley, minced (optional)

Grate the crust of the bread, and chop the crumb into pieces.
Heat the olive oil in a frying pan with the garlic.
Add the bread and continue cooking over low heat until golden. Adjust the salt.
Bring a large pot of salted water to a boil and cook the pici. As soon as they float to the surface, drain them with a slotted spoon and transfer to the bread mixture. Serve hot topped with the grated pecorino, and a sprinkling of minced parsley if desired.

Pici can also be made at home: Mix 1 cup plus 3 tbsps (5½ oz or 150 g) all-purpose flour with 3 tablespoons warm water, and a pinch of salt and knead until smooth and elastic. Let rest for 15 minutes, then roll out small quantities of dough on a wooden pastry board, forming elastic ropes about 8 inches (20 cm) long. To make egg pici, add 1 egg for every 1 lb (500 g) flour.

Preparation time **10 minutes**
Cooking time **20 minutes**
Level **easy**
Wine **Bolgheri Bianco**

pipe with peas and carrots

Ingredients for 4 servings

Pipe:

1 tab of butter, **1** shallot, minced

4 cups (1 litre) hot vegetable broth

1½ cups (7 oz or 200 g) peas

2 carrots, diced, salt and pepper

1 tsp fresh goat's cheese

3 tbsps extra-virgin olive oil

12½ oz (350 g) pipe, lumache or conchiglie pasta

1 tbsp grated Parmesan cheese

Melt the butter in a saucepan and sauté the shallot until soft, adding a little broth if necessary.

Add the peas and cook for 5 minutes, seasoning with salt and pepper. Cover with hot broth and cook until peas are tender.

Puree the peas with the goat's cheese and 2 tablespoons oil, using an immersion blender or in a food processor. Adjust salt and pepper to taste.

Bring a large pot of salted water to a boil and cook the pipe until al dente.

Meanwhile heat 1 tablespoon olive oil in a frying pan and sauté the carrots.

Drain the pasta and mix with the pea puree.

Stir the Parmesan into the pasta and serve with the sautéed carrot cubes.

⌐ For a richer dish, top individual servings of the pasta with shavings of Pecorino Romano and freshly ground black pepper. The carrots can be replaced with diced sun-dried tomato, sautéed briefly with a little oil and water.

Preparation time **10 minutes**
Cooking time **20 minutes**
Level **easy**
Wine **Lugana**

Dried Pasta

linguine with raisins,
pine nuts and cherry tomatoes

Ingredients for 4 servings

Linguine:

3 tbsps raisins

3 tbsps extra-virgin olive oil

5 tbsps pine nuts

5 tbsps breadcrumbs

1 garlic clove

2 cups (10½ oz or 300 g) cherry tomatoes, halved

salt and pepper

14 oz (400 g) linguine

mint, basil and marjoram, minced

Soak the raisins in warm water for at least 15 minutes, then drain and squeeze out excess water.
Meanwhile heat a drizzle of olive oil in a non-stick frying pan and sauté the pine nuts until brown.
Remove the pine nuts from the pan and add the breadcrumbs. Toast, then set aside.
Heat 2 tablespoons olive oil in a frying pan with the garlic. Add the cherry tomatoes, pine nuts, raisins, salt and pepper. Cook over high heat for 5 minutes, then discard the garlic.
Bring a large pot of salted water to a boil and cook the linguine until al dente.
Drain and add to the pan with the sauce.
Toss to combine, then sprinkle with the toasted breadcrumbs and minced herbs.

The pasta can also be finished with a few shavings of ricotta salata cheese.

Preparation time **10 minutes**
Cooking time **5 minutes**
Level **easy**
Wine **Colli di Luni Bianco**

reginette with langoustines and zucchini

Ingredients for 4 servings
Reginette:

14 oz (400 g) langoustines

1¼ cups (5½ oz or 160 g) minced onion, carrot and celery

1 garlic clove, smashed

3 tbsps extra-virgin olive oil

1/2 dried red chili pepper

3 baby zucchini, cut into strips

salt and pepper

8 squash blossoms, chopped

12½ oz (350 g) reginette or pappardelle pasta

Shell the langoustines, reserving the heads and shells. Chop the meat.
Brown the heads and shells in a frying pan with the onion, carrot and celery, cover with water and simmer for 1 hour. Strain the broth.
Sauté the garlic in the olive oil and crumble in the chili pepper. Add the zucchini, season with salt and pepper, and add the langoustine meat.
Sauté briefly, then add the langoustine broth, squash blossoms, salt and pepper.
Bring a pot of salted water to a boil, cook the pasta until al dente, drain and toss with the sauce.

This dish can also be made with small ridged ditalini instead of a long pasta. Cut the zucchini into a small dice instead of strips, and serve the pasta in a wide glass or china bowls.

Preparation time **15 minutes**
Cooking time **1 hour 20 minutes**
Level **easy**
Wine **Val d'Aosta Chardonnay**

tagliolini with caviar
over john dory with pesto

Ingredients for 4 servings

Pesto:

1 bunch of basil

5 tbsps light extra-virgin olive oil

5 tbsps pine nuts, salt and pepper

Pasta:

3 cups (750 ml) fish broth

1 pinch of saffron

2 oz (60 g) rice tagliolini or spaghetti

1 tbsp caviar

2 tbsps light extra-virgin olive oil

Fish:

1 large John Dory fish, filleted, or fillets of another firm, white-fleshed fish

John Dory fish can be refrigerated for a day or two, and in fact if it has just been caught, it will actually improve after a day.

Make the pesto by pureeing all the ingredients in a food processor. Bring the fish broth to a boil with the saffron. Remove 1 cup (250 ml) and chill in the refrigerator. Cook the tagliolini in the boiling fish broth until al dente, then drain and immerse in the chilled broth until cold. Drain and toss with the caviar and a little extra-virgin olive oil.

Cut the fish fillets into diamond shapes, then toss with the pesto. Serve topped with nests of tagliolini.

Preparation time **25 minutes**
Cooking time **35 minutes**
Level **easy**
Wine **Riviera Ligure di Ponente Pigato**

fusilli with zucchini and pancetta

Ingredients for 4 servings

Fusilli:

2 tbsps extra-virgin olive oil

5½ oz (150 g) smoked pancetta
or bacon, diced

3 zucchini, thinly sliced

salt and pepper

13½ oz (380 g) fusilli

shaved ricotta salata or Parmesan
cheese (optional)

Heat the olive oil in a large frying pan and brown
the pancetta or bacon.
Add the zucchini and sauté for 10 minutes.
Season to taste with salt and pepper, remove from
the heat and set aside.
Meanwhile, cook the fusilli in boiling salted water
until al dente.
Drain and transfer the pasta to the pan with the zucchini.
Toss the pasta in the pan to coat with the sauce.
Serve immediately, with shavings of ricotta salata
or Parmesan, if desired.

Try substituting the pancetta
with the same quantity of
thinly sliced speck.

Preparation time **10 minutes**
Cooking time **10 minutes**
Level **easy**
Wine **Sicilia Chardonnay**

spaghetti with tomatoes and roasted pepper

Ingredients for 4 servings
Spaghetti:

1 red bell pepper

4 San Marzano or plum tomatoes

3 tbsps extra-virgin olive oil

1 garlic clove, smashed
fresh basil

dried red chili pepper

salt

11½ oz (320 g) spaghetti

Roast the bell pepper over the open flame of a gas cooker or under a broiler.
Close in a plastic bag to steam. Once cooled, peel and deseed. Cut into strips and set aside.
Blanch the tomatoes in boiling water for about 30 seconds, then peel, deseed and cut into strips.
Heat 2 tablespoons olive oil in a frying pan with the garlic, basil and chili. Add the tomatoes and pepper strips, season with salt and cook over high heat for about 6-7 minutes.
Meanwhile bring a large pot of salted water to a boil and cook the spaghetti until al dente.
Drain and toss with the sauce in the frying pan, adding more basil and a little extra-virgin olive oil.

San Marzano tomatoes have a distinctive elongated shape and make the best canned tomatoes. They come from an area near Naples.

Preparation time **15 minuti**
Cooking time **15 minuti**
Level **facile**
Wine **Aglianico del Taburno**

soy spaghetti stir-fried with seafood and vegetables

Ingredients for 4 servings
Soy Spaghetti:

4 small baby squid, **1** egg

salt and pepper

3 tbsps extra-virgin olive oil

1 spring onion, minced

1/2 cup (3 oz or 80 g) fresh spring peas

1 carrot, julienned

1 cup (3 oz or 80 g) shredded Savoy cabbage heart

1/2 cup (120 ml) hot vegetable broth

10 shrimp, peeled and halved

parsley, minced

12½ oz (350 g) soy spaghetti

Clean the squid under running water, removing the central bone and the dark skin.
Open them up and cut into thin strips.
Beat the egg with salt and pepper.
Heat a small non-stick pan and make an omelet with the egg. Slice it into thin strips and set aside.
Heat the olive oil in a wok and sauté the spring onion.
Add the peas and then the carrot and the cabbage.
Season with salt and pepper, add a little hot broth, and continue cooking. When almost done, add the shrimp and squid and sprinkle with parsley. Continue cooking until the seafood is cooked through, then remove from the heat. Bring a large pot of water to a boil and add the remaining vegetable broth.
Cook the spaghetti until al dente, then drain and toss in the wok with the vegetables and seafood.
Sauté over high heat, add the sliced omelet and serve immediately.

A wok is a round-bottomed iron cooking vessel, particularly used in Chinese cuisine. It can get very hot, and allows foods which have been cut into small pieces to be cooked very quickly.

Preparation time **25 minutes**
Cooking time **10 minutes**
Level **easy**
Wine **Alto Adige Chardonnay**

rice spaghetti with mixed seafood

Ingredients for 4 servings
Rice Spaghetti:

1 lb (500 g) mixed clams,
mussels and cockles

salt

10 cherry tomatoes

3 tbsps extra-virgin olive oil

2 garlic cloves, smashed

1/2 dried red chili pepper, crumbled

parsley, minced

12½ oz (350 g) rice spaghetti

Wash the seafood. Keep the different varieties separate
and clean them carefully, debearding the mussels
and scrubbing the clams and cockles.
Let them sit in separate containers of cold water with
a teaspoon of salt in each container.
Quarter the cherry tomatoes and remove the seeds.
Heat the olive oil with the garlic and chili in a large frying
pan and sauté until the garlic is golden.
Add the clams, then the cockles, then the mussels,
and cover the pan. Continue cooking over high heat until
the shells have all opened.
Add the tomatoes and a little salt. Sprinkle with parsley
and cook for 2 minutes. Discard all the shells.
Bring a large pot of salted water to a boil and cook
the spaghetti until al dente.
Drain and toss with the sauce in the pan.
Serve immediately.

Rice spaghetti is good for people with
a gluten or wheat intolerance as it is
made only from gluten-free rice flour.
The pasta is quite elastic and needs a
very short cooking time. It pairs well
with fish and vegetables.

Preparation time **20 minutes**
Cooking time **10 minutes**
Level **easy**
Wine **Lugana**

spaghetti with chianti classico

Ingredients for 4 servings

Spaghetti:

1 small leek, 1/2 minced and 1/2 julienned

1 tab of butter

3/4 cup (180 ml) Chianti Classico wine

1 tbsp sugar

salt

11 oz (320 g) spaghetti

2 oz (50 g) aged pecorino, shaved

Blanch the julienned leek in boiling water, then drain and set aside.

Melt the butter in a saucepan and sauté the minced leek over low heat, adding a little water to soften it.

Add the wine and sugar and simmer for 15 minutes to reduce the mixture and obtain a syrupy sauce.

Bring a large pot of salted water to the boil and cook the spaghetti until al dente. Drain.

Shape the spaghetti into 4 nests using a fork and a cup, rolling the spaghetti around the fork inside the cup, and arrange the nests on serving plates.

Drizzle over the Chianti sauce and garnish with shavings of pecorino and the julienned leek.

Chianti Classico is a red wine from Tuscany made from Sangiovese grapes. It pairs well with red meat dishes (roast suckling pork, Fiorentina steak) and typical central Italian cured meats and cheeses like Colonnata lardo and semi-aged Tuscan Pecorino. It should be served at 64-68°F (18-20°C).

Preparation time **15 minutes**
Cooking time **25 minutes**
Level **easy**
Wine **Chianti Classico**

mushroom tagliatelle with herb butter

Ingredients for 4 servings

Tagliatelle:

7 tbsps (3½ oz or 100 g) butter, softened

thyme, minced

chives, minced

3-4 fennel seeds

8 cups (2 l) light broth (chicken or vegetable)

14 oz (400 g) mushroom-flavored tagliatelle

1/2 cup (1½ oz or 40 g) chopped almonds

Pound the fennel seeds in a mortar and pestle or with a meat tenderizer.
Spread the butter on a piece of parchment paper to form a thin, even layer. Sprinkle the herbs and fennel seeds over the butter and roll up the paper. Refrigerate the roll.
Bring the broth to a boil in a large pot.
Add the tagliatelle and boil until al dente.
Meanwhile, remove the butter roll from the refrigerator, take the butter out of the parchment paper and break it into little pieces.
Drain the pasta and add the herb butter.
Garnish with almonds. Serve immediately.

Mushroom tagliatelle are made with ground dried mushrooms mixed into the dough. They can be found in specialty stores.

Preparation time **10 minutes**
Cooking time **10 minutes**
Level **easy**
Wine **Alto Adige Merlot**

spaghetti with fresh tomatoes and pancetta

Ingredients for 4 servings
Spaghetti:

3 tbsps extra-virgin olive oil

1 onion, minced

3½ oz (100 g) pancetta, or bacon diced

3 tomatoes, blanched, peeled and diced

salt and pepper

fresh marjoram

14 oz (400 g) spaghetti

grated Pecorino cheese (optional)

Heat the olive oil in a large frying pan and sauté the onion.
Add the pancetta and brown briefly.
Add the tomatoes and cook for a few minutes.
Season to taste with salt and pepper and add
the marjoram leaves.
Boil the spaghetti in abundant salted water and drain
when al dente.
Transfer the pasta to the frying pan with the sauce
and sauté briefly, tossing to coat.
Serve hot, topped with grated Pecorino if desired.

Try substituting the grated
pecorino with thinly shaved
ricotta salata.

Preparation time **5 minutes**
Cooking time **15 minutes**
Level **easy**
Wine **Colli Perugini Rosato**

tagliatelle and braised veal in mushroom sauce

Ingredients for 4 servings
Tagliatelle:

1 veal roast (about 2 lb or 1 kg)

all-purpose flour

3 tbsps extra-virgin olive oil

1 onion, peeled

mustard

5 fresh porcini mushrooms

7 tbsps milk

1 tab of butter

salt

9 oz (250 g) egg tagliatelle

Dust the veal with flour. Heat the olive oil in a large saucepan and brown the veal.
When it is well browned all over, add the whole onion and mustard, cover and cook for 1 hour over low heat. Clean the porcini mushrooms with damp paper towels, then slice and set aside.
When the veal is cooked through, remove from the pan and keep warm. Discard the onion.
Add the mushrooms to the same pan and sauté.
Add the milk, and if the sauce seems too liquid, some flour. Once the mushrooms are cooked, remove from the heat and stir in the butter.
Bring a large pot of salted water to a boil and cook the tagliatelle until al dente. Slice the veal.
Drain the tagliatelle and toss in the pan with the mushroom sauce and the slices of veal.

The fresh mushrooms can be replaced by 1 oz (30 g) dried porcini, soaked in warm water before using.

Preparation time **20 minutes**
Cooking time **1 hour 30 minutes**
Level **easy**
Wine **Dolcetto di Dogliani**

rye tagliatelle with porcini mushrooms

Ingredients for 4 servings
Rye Tagliatelle:

3-4 fresh porcini mushrooms

3 tbsps extra-virgin olive oil

1 garlic clove

1/2 red chili pepper, minced

parsley and thyme, minced

salt

12½ oz (350 g) dried rye tagliatelle

2 tbsps heavy cream

Clean the porcini with damp paper towels and cut off the earthy part of the stalk.
Thinly slice the mushrooms and set aside.
Heat the olive oil in a frying pan with the garlic and chili and sauté gently until the garlic is golden.
Add the mushrooms and sauté for 10 minutes, then sprinkle with parsley and thyme.
Bring a large pot of salted water to a boil and cook the tagliatelle until al dente.
Add 1 ladleful of the pasta cooking water and the cream to the mushrooms and simmer until reduced.
Drain the tagliatelle and toss in the pan with the sauce.

Preparation time **15 minutes**
Cooking time **20 minutes**
Level **easy**
Wine **Alto Adige Pinot Nero**

penne with roast pepper cream and almonds

Ingredients for 4 servings

Penne:

1/2 yellow bell pepper

1/2 red bell pepper

3 tbsps extra-virgin olive oil

1 onion, minced

3/4 cup (180 ml) vegetable broth

salt and pepper

2 tbsps heavy cream

12½ oz (350 g) whole-wheat or farro penne

2 tbsps slivered almonds, toasted

Roast the bell peppers under the broiler, then wrap in plastic wrap and let sit for 10-15 minutes.
Unwrap, peel, deseed and cut into thin strips.
Heat the olive oil and sauté the onion.
Add the roast peppers and vegetable broth. Lower the heat and cook for 15 minutes. Salt and pepper to taste and then puree in a food processor with the cream.
Bring a large pot of salted water to a boil and cook the penne until al dente.
Drain and toss with the pepper cream.
Garnish with almonds and serve hot.

Almonds stay fresh inside their shell, but once shelled they should be protected as much as possible from light, air and heat. If they are being stored for a long time, they can also be frozen.

Preparation time **10 minutes**
Cooking time **30 minutes**
Level **easy**
Wine **Lagrein Rosato**

penne with gorgonzola and pistachios

Ingredients for 4 servings

Penne:

1/2 cup (2 oz or 50 g) shelled pistachios

2 tbsps (1 oz or 30 g) butter

2 tbsps extra-virgin olive oil

5½ oz (150 g) Gorgonzola cheese, chopped

7 tbsps heavy cream

1 bunch of chives, chopped

salt and pepper

nutmeg

12½ oz (350 g) ridged penne

Blanch the pistachios in boiling water for 30 seconds. Drain and rub with a clean kitchen towel to remove the skins. Coarsely chop the nuts.
Heat the butter and olive oil in a frying pan.
Add the pistachios and sauté for a few minutes.
Add the Gorgonzola and cream and stir until smooth.
Remove from the heat, add the chives and season with salt, pepper and freshly grated nutmeg to taste.
Bring a large pot of salted water to a boil and cook the penne until al dente.
Drain and toss with the sauce. Serve hot.

Preparation time **20 minutes**
Cooking time **20 minutes**
Level **easy**
Wine **Lagrein Rosato**

kamut farfalle with pumpkin and mushroom ragù

Ingredients for 4 servings

Kamut Farfalle:

1 spring onion

3 tbsps extra-virgin olive oil

2¼ cups (9 oz or 250 g) diced pumpkin or other winter squash

salt and pepper

2⅔ cups (7 oz or 200 g) sliced mushrooms

1/3 cup (2 oz or 50 g) pitted black olives, chopped

10½ oz (300 g) kamut farfalle

fresh basil leaves

grated Parmesan cheese (optional)

Thinly slice the white part of the spring onion. Mince the green part and keep separate.
Heat the olive oil and sauté the white spring onion.
Add the pumpkin and salt and cook for 5 minutes over medium heat.
Add the mushrooms and raise the heat. Sauté briefly, then add a little water and cook, covered, for 10 minutes.
Add the green part of the spring onion and the olives and remove from the heat.
Bring a large pot of salted water to a boil and cook the farfalle for the length of time indicated on the package. Drain and transfer to the pan with the sauce. Toss and sauté for a few minutes, then add the basil. Sprinkle with grated Parmesan cheese, if desired, then serve immediately.

Kamut can be found as a grain, ground into flour, or in couscous, pasta or cookies. It has a higher percentage of protein than wheat and is rich in minerals and vitamin E, which has an antioxidant effect.

Preparation time **20 minutes**
Cooking time **25 minutes**
Level **easy**
Wine **Lagrein Rosato**

corn gnocchi with tuna and tofu

Ingredients for 4 servings
Gnocchi:

5½ oz (150 g) plain tofu

salt

2 tbsps extra-virgin olive oil

2½ tbsps salted capers, rinsed

12½ oz (350 g) dried corn gnocchi

1/2 cup (2 oz or 60 g) pitted
green olives, chopped

5½ oz (150 g) tuna in oil, drained
fresh marjoram, minced

Boil the tofu in lightly salted water for 10 minutes.
Drain and place in a blender with the olive oil, capers
and a pinch of salt.
Puree, adding water if necessary, until smooth and fluid.
Bring a large pot of salted water to a boil and cook
the pasta until al dente.
Drain and toss with the tofu puree.
Fold in the olives, tuna and marjoram.
Stir carefully and serve.

Tofu is a Chinese and Japanese specialty
which can be found in most supermarkets
and Asian markets. It is sometimes called
"soy cheese" because it looks like cheese
and is made from curdling a milky liquid
produced from soy beans.

Preparation time **15 minutes**
Cooking time **20 minutes**
Level **easy**
Wine **Sicilia Chardonnay**

farro fusilli with feta and asparagus

Ingredients for 4 servings
Farro Fusilli:

20 asparagus spears (about
10½ oz or 300 g)

4 tbsps extra-virgin olive oil

1 shallot, thinly sliced

1/2 cup (120 ml) dry white wine

5½ oz (150 g) feta cheese, crumbled

salt and black pepper

11½ oz (320 g) farro fusilli

Slice the asparagus stalks along the diagonal and keep the tips whole.
Heat a little of the olive oil in a frying pan and sauté the shallot until golden.
Add the white wine and let cook off for a few minutes.
Add the feta and let it melt over low heat.
Puree the sauce in a blender or with an immersion blender, adding a little water if necessary, and set aside.
Bring a large pot of salted water to a boil and cook the fusilli and asparagus together.
Drain and toss with the feta sauce.
Sprinkle with black pepper and drizzle with olive oil.
Serve hot.

Feta is a cheese originally from Greece. Traditionally it is made with goat's or sheep's milk, but most of what is found on the market today is made from cow's milk. Feta is excellent crumbled over fresh summer salads.

Preparation time **5 minutes**
Cooking time **10 minutes**
Level **easy**
Wine **Val d'Aosta Pinot Bianco**

seaweed tagliatelle with fennel and salmon

Ingredients for 4 servings

Tagliatelle:

4 tbsps extra-virgin olive oil

2 spring onions, chopped

7 oz (200 g) fresh salmon fillet, chopped

salt and pepper

1 fennel bulb, thinly sliced

10 oz (280 g) seaweed-flavored tagliatelle

1 dill sprig, minced

Heat 3 tablespoons olive oil in a frying pan and sauté the spring onions until soft.
Add the salmon and cook over low heat for 5 minutes.
Season with salt and pepper.
Bring a large pot of salted water to a boil.
Blanch the fennel, drain with a slotted spoon and add to the salmon mixture.
Use the same water to cook the tagliatelle until al dente.
Drain and add to the sauce.
Add the dill and a drizzle of olive oil and serve.

The fennel can be replaced with 2 baby zucchini, julienned and sautéed in the pan with the spring onion instead of blanched.

Preparation time **10 minutes**
Cooking time **10 minutes**
Level **easy**
Wine **Ortrugo**

buckwheat pasta with peppers and fava beans

Ingredients for 4 servings

Pasta:

1 red bell pepper

1⅓ cup (7 oz or 200 g) shelled fava beans

4 tbsps extra-virgin olive oil

1 red onion, thinly sliced

salt and pepper

11½ oz (320 g) short buckwheat pasta (rigatoni, penne or fusilli)

fresh basil leaves, torn

Roast the bell pepper over an open flame or under the broiler until completely blackened. Close in a paper bag for 5 minutes, then peel, deseed, rinse and dice. Blanch the fava beans in boiling water for 1 minute. Drain and peel off the outer skin.

Heat the olive oil in a frying pan and sauté the onion with a pinch of salt. Add the bell pepper and fava beans. Season with salt, add a little water and cook, covered, for 10 minutes.

Bring a large pot of salted water to a boil and cook the pasta until al dente.

Drain and add the pan with the sauce.

Sauté for a few minutes to blend the flavors, then add the basil and a sprinkling of pepper and serve.

Basil should always be torn by hand, and never cut with a steel knife, which can alter its flavor.

Preparation time **20 minutes**
Cooking time **25 minutes**
Level **easy**
Wine **Friuli Isonzo Sauvignon**

spaghetti with shrimp and asparagus in spicy tomato sauce

Ingredients for 4 servings

Spaghetti:

3 tbsps extra-virgin olive oil

2 red chili peppers, minced

3/4 cup (7 oz or 200 g) ready-made tomato sauce

1 garlic clove

20 shrimp, shelled

24 asparagus tips

1/2 cup (120 ml) brandy

salt

12½ oz (350 g) spaghettini (thin spaghetti)

Heat 1 tablespoon olive oil in a frying pan and sauté the chili peppers. Add the tomato sauce and let simmer for 15 minutes.
Meanwhile heat 2 tablespoons oil in another frying pan and sauté the unpeeled garlic clove until golden.
Add the shrimp, sauté briefly, then add the brandy.
Add the asparagus and cook for 10 minutes.
Bring a large pot of salted water to a boil and cook the spaghettini until al dente. Drain and transfer to the frying pan with the shrimp and asparagus.
Arrange on serving plates and serve topped with a spoonful of the spicy tomato sauce.

The tomato sauce can be replaced with the same quantity of cherry tomatoes. Mince a shallot and sauté in 1 tablespoon oil, then add the quartered cherry tomatoes. Simmer until cooked through, seasoning with dried chili pepper flakes.

Preparation time **20 minutes**
Cooking time **10 minutes**
Level **easy**
Wine **Bianco d'Alcamo**

paccheri with vernaccia and pheasant ragù

Ingredients for 4 servings

Paccheri:

1 pheasant

3 tbsps extra-virgin olive oil

1¼ cup (5½ oz or 150 g) minced celery, carrot and onion

1 garlic clove, smashed

3 sage leaves, minced

2½ oz (70 g) ground pork

3/4 cup (180 ml) Vernaccia or other white wine

salt and pepper

1/2 tsp tomato paste

1/2 cup (120 ml) beef broth

2 tbsps chopped tomatoes

14 oz (400 g) Gragnano paccheri or large rigatoni pasta

Clean the pheasant, removing the entrails, and cut into pieces.

Heat the oil in a saucepan and sauté the celery, carrot, onion, garlic and sage until soft.

Add the pork, then the pheasant pieces. Pour over the wine and cook over high heat for 10 minutes. Season with salt and pepper.

Dissolve the tomato paste in a little broth and add together with the tomatoes to the sauce. Remove from the heat.

Take out the pheasant pieces, let cool and remove the meat from the bones.

Chop the meat and return to the pan.

Add the broth, season with salt and pepper and cook over low heat until the sauce thickens.

Bring a large pot of salted water to the boil and cook the pasta until al dente.

Drain and toss gently with the ragù. Serve immediately.

Preparation time **30 minutes**
Cooking time **20 minutes**
Level **easy**
Wine **Nero d'Avola**

penne with crab and tomato

Ingredients for 4 servings
Penne:

2 lb (1 kg) crabs

4 cups (1 litre) water

2 lb (1 kg) canned plum tomatoes

3 tbsps extra-virgin olive oil

3 garlic cloves, minced

sage, minced

red chili pepper, minced

salt

10½ oz (300 g) ridged penne

2 tabs of butter

parsley, minced

Wash the crabs well and place in a saucepan with the water and tomatoes. Bring to a boil and cook, uncovered, for about 20 minutes.
Remove the crabs with a slotted spoon, crack them and remove the meat, leaving the claws intact.
Heat the olive oil in a non-stick frying pan and sauté the garlic, sage and chili.
Transfer the mixture to the saucepan with the water and tomatoes and add the crab meat and claws.
Season with salt and cook for about an hour, until the sauce is thickened.
Bring a large pot of salted water to a boil and cook the penne until al dente. Drain and transfer to the sauce. Stir in the butter and serve, sprinkled with parsley.

Preparation time **35 minutes**
Cooking time **1 hour 20 minutes**
Level **medium**
Wine **Bianco Vergine Valdichiana**

spaghetti with parsley and pecorino

Ingredients for 4 servings
Spaghetti:

salt and pepper

1 lb (500 g) thick spaghetti

4 tbsps extra-virgin olive oil

3 garlic cloves, thickly sliced

5 tbsps grated Pecorino cheese

parsley, minced

Bring a large pot of salted water to a boil and add the spaghetti.
Meanwhile heat the olive oil in a non-stick frying pan and sauté the garlic until golden.
Drain the spaghetti when al dente and transfer to the pan with the garlic.
Season with salt and pepper and stir well.
Sauté for a few minutes then transfer to serving plates and top with Pecorino and parsley.

Preparation time **5 minutes**
Cooking time **12 minutes**
Level **easy**
Wine **Bianco di Pitigliano**

linguine with pesto, green beans and potatoes

Ingredients for 4 servings

Pesto:

40 basil leaves, **2** tbsps pine nuts

1 tbsp grated Pecorino cheese

4 tbsps grated Parmesan cheese

5 tbsps extra-virgin olive oil

1 garlic clove, salt

Linguine:

salt, **2** potatoes, diced

3½ oz (100 g) green beans, topped and tailed

1 lb (450 g) linguine

grated Parmesan cheese (optional)

Puree all the pesto ingredients in a food processor.
Bring a large pot of salted water to a boil and add the potatoes and green beans.
When the water returns to a boil add the linguine.
As soon as the pasta is cooked, drain together with the vegetables, using a slotted spoon so the cooking water is reserved.
Chop the green beans. Place the pasta, potatoes and green beans in a large serving bowl.
Dilute the pesto with 1 tablespoon of the pasta cooking water and add to the linguine.
Stir well and serve hot, sprinkled with extra grated Parmesan if desired.

Other pasta shapes can be used in this recipe, such as dried trenette. The pasta can also be sprinkled with Pecorino at the end, or with a mixture of Pecorino and Parmesan.

Preparation time **30 minutes**
Cooking time **25 minutes**
Level **easy**
Wine **Riviera Ligure di Ponente Pigato**

fresh pasta

Pasta

orecchiette with saffron fennel and baby spinach

Ingredients for 4 servings
Orecchiette:

2 medium-small fennel bulbs

1 pinch of saffron

salt and pepper

3 tbsps extra-virgin olive oil

1 garlic clove, smashed

1 handful of baby spinach leaves, shredded

1/2 cup (120 ml) milk

5½ oz (150 g) Camembert cheese, chopped

14 oz (400 g) fresh orecchiette pasta

grated Parmesan cheese (optional)

Trim the fennel, removing the hard base and the green leaves, and cut into wedges.
Place enough water to cover the fennel in a saucepan and add the saffron and salt. Bring to a boil, then add the fennel and cook for about 15 minutes, until tender but still al dente.
Drain. Heat the olive oil in a frying pan with the garlic and add first the fennel and then the spinach.
Cook for 1 minute and season with salt and pepper.
Add the milk and the cheese and stir until melted.
Bring a large pot of salted water to a boil and cook the orecchiette. Drain and transfer to the pan with the sauce and stir well to combine.
Serve sprinkled with grated Parmesan, if desired.

Did you know that fennel was once served at the end of the meal as a fruit? This vegetable is extremely popular these days and can be found in soups, gratins and salads.

Preparation time **20 minutes**
Cooking time **35 minutes**
Level **easy**
Wine **Bianco d'Alcamo Riserva**

tagliatelle with fennel, spinach and cannellini beans

Ingredients for 4 servings

Tagliatelle:

1 fennel bulb

3 tbsps (1½ oz or 40 g) butter

2 tbsps extra-virgin olive oil

1 shallot, minced

3/4 cup (180 ml) vegetable broth

salt and pepper

3½ oz (100 g) fresh spinach leaves

1/2 cup (3 oz or 80 g) cooked cannellini beans

14 oz (400 g) fresh egg tagliatelle

2 oz (50 g) aged Pecorino cheese, shaved

Trim the fennel, removing the fibrous outer layer, and cut the rest into thin slices.
Heat the butter and olive oil in a saucepan and sauté the shallot over low heat. Add the fennel and cook for 10 minutes, adding broth little by little.
Season with salt and pepper to taste. Blanch the spinach in boiling salted water. Drain and add to the fennel.
Puree the spinach-fennel mixture with half the beans in a food processor and adjust salt and pepper.
Halve the remaining beans.
Bring a large pot of salted water to a boil and cook the tagliatelle. Drain and return them to the saucepan with the puree and the halved beans.
Stir and serve, topped with Pecorino shavings.

Pecorino is a generic term to indicate cheese made from sheep's milk. Some of the best known Pecorino cheeses are Pecorino Romano, Pecorino Toscano and Pecorino Sardo, from Rome, Tuscany and Sardinia respectively.

Preparation time **10 minutes**
Cooking time **25 minutes**
Level **easy**
Wine **Vermentino di Gallura**

Fresh Pasta

green and yellow maltagliati

Ingredients for 4 servings
Maltagliati:

2 cups (8.8 oz or 250 g)
plain flour

1/2 cup (120 ml) water

2 eggs

salt

Sauce:

2 tbsps extra-virgin olive oil

1 tab of butter, **1** shallot, minced

6 aspargus spears, peeled
and thinly sliced

2 zucchini, deseeded and diced

1/2 cup (120 ml) hot vegetable broth

salt and pepper

2 boiled eggs, yolks only

Adding the boiled egg yolk gives
a creaminess and colours
the asparagus cooking liquid,
and makes the pasta creamier.

Mix the flour, water, eggs and a little salt to obtain
a smooth dough. Let rest for 30 minutes.
Roll out the dough and cut into strips of around
5-inches (12 cm).
Heat the oil and butter in a saucepan and sauté
the shallot. Add asparagus, then zucchini and sauté
for 2 minutes. Add hot broth and continue cooking until
vegetables are tender, seasoning with salt and pepper.
Crumble the yolks into the pan.
Bring a large pot of salted water to the boil and cook
the pasta. Drain and toss with the sauce.
Serve immediately.

Preparazione **30 minutes**
Cottura **15 minutes**
Esecuzione **easy**
Vino **Lugana**

maltagliati with quails, truffle and porcini

Ingredients for 4 servings
Maltagliati:

3 tbsps extra-virgin olive oil

1/2 yellow onion, minced

1/2 celery stalk, minced

1/2 carrot, minced, sage leaves

3½ oz (100 g) ground pork

2 quails, quartered

1/2 cup (120 ml) white wine

1/2 tbsp raisins, **1/2** tbsp pine nuts

salt and pepper

1 large porcini mushroom, sliced

1 garlic clove, unpeeled

1/2 black truffle, shaved

1 lb (450 g) fresh egg pasta dough
or fresh lasagna sheets

Heat 2 tablespoons olive oil in a large saucepan and sauté the onion, celery and carrot with the sage.
Add the pork and brown for 5 minutes. Add the quails and wine, let evaporate and cook for 15 minutes.
Remove the quails from the saucepan, debone and chop the meat. Return it to the pan with the raisins and pine nuts and season with salt and pepper.
Heat 1 tablespoon olive oil in a frying pan and sauté the mushrooms slices with the garlic. Season with salt and pepper.
Roll out the egg pasta dough and cut into irregular shapes, or cut the lasagna sheets into irregular shapes.
Bring a large pot of salted water to a boil and cook the pasta until al dente.
Drain, add to the pan with the quail and toss.
Serve the maltagliati topped with the sautéed mushrooms and truffle.

Preparation time **20 minutes**
Cooking time **30 minutes**
Level **medium**
Wine **Gattinara**

orecchiette with spicy, creamy greens

Ingredients for 4 servings

Orecchiette:

1½ cups (10 oz or 280 g) semolina flour

salt

Sauce:

5½ oz (150 g) fresh spinach leaves

5½ oz (150 g) Swiss chard, white stalks trimmed off

salt and pepper

3 tbsps extra-virgin olive oil

1 garlic clove, sliced

1 dried red chili pepper, crumbled

1 tbsp grated Parmesan cheese

3½ oz (100 g) Feta cheese, crumbled

Swiss chard is the same species as the beet, but they are grown for the leaves while beets are grown primarily for their large red or yellow roots.

Mix the semolina and salt with enough water to form a dough. Cover and let rest for 20 minutes.
Blanch the spinach and Swiss chard in boiling salted water for 5 minutes. Drain and squeeze out excess water. Heat the olive oil in a small frying pan and sauté the garlic and chile.
Add the mixture to the cooked greens and puree in a food processor. Add water if necessary and adjust salt and pepper. Blend in the Parmesan and Feta.
Divide the dough into small portions and roll them in ropes. Cut off equal-sized pieces and press each one with the thumb on a floured work surface to create orecchiette. Bring a large pot of salted water to a boil and cook the orecchiette. Drain and toss with the sauce.

Preparation time **35 minutes**
Cooking time **15 minutes**
Level **easy**
Wine **Alto Adige Pinot Bianco**

pappardelle with duck and porcini ragù

Ingredients for 4 servings

Pappardelle:

2⅓ cups plus **1** tbsp (10½ oz or 300 g) all-purpose flour

3 eggs

Sauce:

1 oz (25 g) dried porcini mushrooms

3 tbsps extra-virgin olive oil

1 tab of butter, **1** garlic clove, smashed

2/3 cup (3 oz or 80 g) minced celery, carrot and onion

9 oz (250 g) skinned and deboned duck leg or breast meat, diced

1/2 cup (120 ml) red wine, salt

1 cup (7 oz or 200 g) peeled canned plum tomatoes, roughly chopped

1 bay leaf, **2-3** peppercorns

2 cloves, ground in a mortar and pestle

3/4 cup (180 g) vegetable broth

5 tbsps grated Parmesan cheese

2 tbsps minced mixed fresh herbs

Mix the flour and eggs together to make a smooth dough. Cover with plastic wrap and let rest for 30 minutes. Meanwhile soak the dried porcini in warm water until soft, then drain and squeeze out excess liquid.
Heat the olive oil and garlic in a saucepan and sauté the celery, carrot and onion.
Add the duck and the porcini and then the red wine. Once it has cooked off, add the tomatoes.
Season with a pinch of salt, bay, peppercorns and cloves. Add the broth and cook for 25-30 minutes.
Roll out the pasta dough and cut out long, thick strips of pappardelle using a rolling cutter.
Bring a large pot of salted water to a boil and cook the pasta. Drain when al dente and add to the sauce. Add the Parmesan, butter and herbs.
Stir and serve immediately.

Preparation time **40 minutes**
Cooking time **30 minutes**
Level **medium**
Wine **Rosso di Montalcino**

Fresh Pasta

passatelli with peas, prosciutto and shrimp

Ingredients for 4 servings
Passatelli:

2½ cups (10½ oz or 300 g)
breadcrumbs

2 cups (7 oz or 200 g) grated
Parmesan cheese

5 eggs, grated zest
of **1/2** organic lemon

freshly grated nutmeg

8 cups (2 l) beef broth

Sauce:

4 cups (1 lb or 500 g) fresh peas

5 tbsps extra-virgin olive oil

5 tbsps chopped shallot

1 garlic clove, smashed

4 slices of prosciutto

20 large shrimp, shelled and deveined

Mix together all the passatelli ingredients together except for the beef broth. Refrigerate for 30 minutes.
Blanch the peas in boiling water for a few minutes, then drain. Let cool.
Heat 1 tablespoon olive oil in a frying pan and sauté the shallot and garlic. Add the peas and sauté for a minute. Remove the garlic and puree the rest in a food processor. Pass through a sieve then let cool.
Trim the fat off the prosciutto slices then cut them into julienne strips.
Cut the shrimp in half lengthwise. Heat 2 tablespoons olive oil in a frying pan and sauté the shrimp over high heat.
Bring the broth to a boil and then press the dough through a passatelli-making tool or a potato ricer held over the boiling broth, so that long strands fall directly into the broth. Let simmer for a few minutes, then drain.
Compose plates starting with a spoonful of the warm pea cream, then the passatelli, the sautéed shrimp and finally the julienned prosciutto and a drizzle of olive oil.

Preparation time **35 minutes**
Cooking time **15 minutes**
Level **medium**
Wine **Valle d'Aosta Chardonnay**

Julienne is a technique of cutting vegetables into thin strips, which can be used in garnishes, soups or salads.

strozzapreti with zucchini, lemon and mint

Ingredients for 4 servings

Strozzapreti:

3 small, pale-green zucchini

2 tbsps extra-virgin olive oil

1 shallot, minced

salt and pepper

grated zest of **1** organic lemon

2 tbsps heavy cream

12½ oz (360 g) fresh strozzapreti or other short pasta

2 mint sprigs, leaves only

Peel the zucchini with a vegetable peeler and cut the green skin into julienne strips.

Heat the olive oil in a frying pan and sauté the shallot over low heat. Add the zucchini and sauté for 2 minutes. Season to taste with salt and pepper. Add the lemon zest and cream and stir. Remove from the heat.

Bring a large pot of salted water to a boil and cook the strozzapreti.

Drain and transfer to the frying pan with the zucchini. Return briefly to the heat and stir until combined. Add a few mint leaves and serve hot.

134

Biphenyl is a mildly toxic chemical used to protect fresh citrus fruits from molds and fungus. When using the zest or rind of citrus, try to use organic fruit, or rub treated citrus with alcohol and wash it well before use.

Preparation time **10 minutes**
Cooking time **15 minutes**
Level **easy**
Wine **Alto Adige Riesling**

tagliolini with anchovies and zucchini

Ingredients for 4 servings
Tagliolini:

12½ oz (350 g) fresh tagliolini

salt

3 zucchini, sliced into matchsticks

6 anchovy fillets in oil

4 tbsps extra-virgin olive oil

parsley, minced

grated zest of **1** organic lemon

Bring a large pot of salted water to a boil and cook the tagliolini. Add the zucchini to the water 2 minutes before draining the pasta.

Drain the tagliolini and zucchini and transfer to a serving bowl. Add the anchovy fillets and drizzle generously with olive oil.

Top with the minced parsley and grated lemon zest and serve immediately.

For a stronger-flavored pasta, substitute the zucchini with a ready-made truffle cream. Truffles and anchovies make a surprisingly good match.

Preparation time **5 minutes**
Cooking time **6 minutes**
Level **easy**
Wine **Sicilia Inzolia**

tagliatelle with pesto and cherry tomatoes

Ingredients for 4 servings

Tagliatelle:

2⅓ cups plus 1 tbsp
(10½ oz or 300 g) all-purpose flour

3 eggs

Sauce:

1½ cups (7 oz or 200 g)
cherry tomatoes

salt, thyme, minced

3 bunches of basil

1 handful of pine nuts, **1** tbsp walnuts

6 tbsps extra-virgin olive oil

Refrigerate the food processor container and blade
for 20 minutes to avoid overheating the basil while making
the pesto.
Meanwhile mix together the flour and eggs to make
a dough. Roll it out thinly and cut into tagliatelle using
a pasta machine.
Blanch the cherry tomatoes in boiling water for 2 minutes.
Drain, immerse in cold water, drain again and peel.
Dice the tomatoes and place them in a bowl with a pinch
of salt and the thyme.
Puree the basil, pine nuts, walnuts and olive oil, pulsing
the food processor to avoid overheating the blade.
Bring a large pot of salted water to a boil and cook
the tagliatelle.
Drain and toss with the tomatoes and pesto.

The pesto can also be made with
the addition of a bunch of
arugula, plus a sprig of parsley
or thyme to add extra flavor.
The pine nuts can also be
replaced with cashews.

Preparation time **20 minutes**
Cooking time **20 minutes**
Level **easy**
Wine **Gambellara**

tagliatelle with porcini ragù

Ingredients for 4 servings

Tagliatelle:

2⅓ cups plus 1 tbsp (10½ oz or 300 g) all-purpose flour

3 eggs, salt

Sauce:

3 fresh porcini mushrooms (about 9 oz or 250 g)

2 garlic cloves, **2** tomatoes

2 tbsps extra-virgin olive oil

1/2 dried red chili pepper, crumbled

parsley, minced

salt and pepper

Porcini ragù is a classic for autumn and winter. It pairs well with all egg pastas, but particularly tagliatelle and pappardelle. For a variation on the basic recipe, eliminate the tomatoes and replace the parsley with mint.

Mix together the flour, eggs and a pinch of salt to make a dough, then wrap in plastic wrap and refrigerate for 30 minutes.

Clean the mushrooms with damp paper towels and remove the earthy part of the stalk. Cut the mushrooms into small pieces and set aside.

Blanch the tomatoes in boiling water, then drain and immerse in ice water. Drain and peel them. Quarter the tomatoes, remove the seeds and dice the flesh.

Heat the oil with the whole, peeled garlic cloves and the chile. Add the mushrooms and sauté for 3 minutes, sprinkling with the parsley.

Add the tomatoes and a little salt.

Roll the pasta dough out thinly with a pasta machine and then cut into tagliatelle. Bring a large pot of salted water to a boil and cook the tagliatelle for 2 minutes. Drain and transfer to the pan with the sauce.

Season lightly with pepper and toss together over high heat briefly.

Preparation time **30 minutes**
Cooking time **10 minutes**
Level **easy**
Wine **Rossese di Dolceacqua**

buckwheat tagliatelle with favas

Ingredients for 4 servings
Tagliatelle:

1½ cups plus 1½ tbsps (7 oz or 200 g) all-purpose flour

3/4 cup plus 1 tbsp (3½ oz or 100 g) buckwheat flour

3 eggs, salt

Sauce:

2 tbsps extra-virgin olive oil

2 garlic cloves, smashed

1/2 red chili pepper

9 oz (250 g) fava bean pods

3/4 cup (180 ml) vegetable broth

6 tbsps grated semi-aged Pecorino cheese

Garnish:

Pecorino shavings

Fresh favas must be peeled and can then be used like fresh peas. Dried favas must be soaked for a long time and then boiled for a long time, even in a pressure cooker.

Sift the all-purpose and buckwheat flours together and mound on a work surface.
Make a well in the center and break in the eggs.
Add a pinch of salt and work well to obtain a smooth dough. Wrap in plastic wrap and let rest for 20 minutes.
Using a pasta machine, roll out the dough and cut into tagliatelle. Shell and peel the fava beans.
Heat the olive oil in a frying pan, sauté the garlic and chile and then add the favas and broth and cook for 10 minutes over medium heat. Remove the garlic and chile and stir in the grated Pecorino. Bring a pot of salted water to a boil and cook the tagliatelle for 2 minutes.
Drain and add to the pan with the sauce and continue cooking until al dente.
Sprinkle the pasta with Pecorino shavings and serve immediately.

Preparation time **25 minutes**
Cooking time **20 minutes**
Level **easy**
Wine **Alto Adige Santa Maddalena**

farro tagliatelle with truffle cream

Ingredients for 4 servings
Tagliatelle:

1 tbsp extra-virgin olive oil

1/2 white onion, finely minced

1/2 tsp fresh grated ginger

1 black truffle, thinly shaved

1 cup (250 ml) heavy cream

salt and pepper

10½ oz (300 g) fresh farro tagliatelle

1 handful of pine nuts

Heat the olive oil in a frying pan and sauté the onion for a few minutes, adding a little water.
Add the ginger and truffle shavings.
Stir in the cream and let reduce over low heat.
Season to taste with salt and pepper.
Bring a large pot of salted water to a boil and cook the tagliatelle.
Drain and transfer to the pan with the sauce.
Toss to coat and then serve, sprinkled with the pine nuts.

Here's another recipe for a sauce that goes well with farro tagliatelle: Sauté some minced leek in a wok with some olive oil. Crumble a block of tofu with a fork and add to the wok together with 1 tablespoon soy sauce, 10 pitted and halved green olives, thinly sliced fresh ginger and a handful of coarsely chopped walnuts. Toss the cooked pasta with the sauce and serve hot.

Preparation time **10 minutes**
Cooking time **20 minutes**
Level **easy**
Wine **Lagrein Rosato**

Fresh Pasta

144

corn tagliatelle with radicchio, provola and walnuts

Ingredients for 4 servings

Tagliatelle:

1 cup plus 3 tbsps (5½ oz or 150 g) all-purpose flour

3/4 cup plus 2 tbsps (5½ oz or 150 g) finely ground cornmeal

3 eggs, salt, semolina flour

Sauce:

2 tbsps extra-virgin olive oil

1 shallot, minced, salt and pepper

1 head of Treviso radicchio (see note), thinly sliced

1/2 cup (2 oz or 50 g) walnuts, crumbled

3½ oz (100 g) mild provola or Provolone cheese, diced

Treviso radicchio has long, pointed leaves, a dark purple-red color and white ribs. Prize examples can reach up to 1½ feet (50 cm) high. It can be replaced by regular round radicchio in this recipe.

Mix together all the pasta ingredients except the semolina with the fingers then knead with the palms of the hands to make a smooth, uniform dough.
Wrap in plastic wrap and refrigerate for 30 minutes.
Roll the pasta out thinly with a pasta machine and cut tagliatelle. Dust with semolina and lay out on a tray to dry.
Heat the olive oil in a non-stick frying pan and sauté the shallot. Add the radicchio and walnuts. Add a little water, salt and pepper and then stir in the provola.
Bring a large pot of salted water to a boil and cook the tagliatelle for 2 minutes.
Drain and transfer to the frying pan with the sauce.
Stir until the cheese melts, then serve immediately.

Preparation time **30 minutes**
Cooking time **10 minutes**
Level **easy**
Wine **Lagrein Rosato**

tagliatelle with radicchio, arugula and goat's cheese

Ingredients for 4 servings

Tagliatelle:

2⅓ cups plus 1 tbsp (10½ oz or 300 g) all-purpose flour

2 eggs plus 2 egg yolks

salt

Sauce:

2 tbsps extra-virgin olive oil

1/2 white onion, minced

1 head of radicchio, preferably Treviso, shredded

1 bunch of arugula, shredded

salt and pepper

5½ oz (150 g) goat's milk cheese

nutmeg

1 tbsp grated Parmesan cheese

Goat's milk cheese is also known by its French name, chèvre (French for "goat"). Use a fresh, soft, spreadable goat's cheese which will melt easily for this recipe.

Mound the flour on a work surface and make a well in the center. Place the eggs, egg yolks and a pinch of salt in the middle and mix together to form a smooth and uniform dough. Wrap in plastic wrap and refrigerate. Heat the olive oil in a saucepan and sauté the onion. Add the radicchio and arugula and brown slightly, then add a ladleful of water. Lightly season with salt and pepper then remove from the heat and stir in the goat's cheese and some freshly grated nutmeg.
Stir until the cheese has melted.
Roll the pasta dough out thinly and cut into tagliatelle with a pasta machine.
Bring a large pot of salted water to a boil and cook the tagliatelle. Drain them and transfer to the pan with the sauce. Sauté briefly to combine and to reduce the sauce, then sprinkle with Parmesan and serve hot.

Preparation time **35 minutes**
Cooking time **15 minutes**
Level **easy**
Wine **Gambellara**

arezzo-style pappardelle
with duck ragù

Ingredients for 4 servings
Pappardelle:
2-3 tomatoes (about 10½ oz or 300 g)
1/4 cup (2 oz or 60 g) butter
1 duck
salt
1/2 onion, minced
1/2 carrot, minced
1/2 celery stalk, minced
1½ oz (40 g) prosciutto, diced
nutmeg
2 cups (500 ml) beef broth
14 oz (400 g) fresh pappardelle

Blanch the tomatoes, drain, peel and pass through a sieve.
Melt the butter in a saucepan and brown the duck, turning frequently, until evenly colored.
Remove from the heat, debone and chop into small pieces. Season with salt.
In the same pan, sauté the onion, carrot, celery and prosciutto, then add the tomatoes with a grating of nutmeg. Add the duck. Continue cooking over low heat for 40 minutes, stirring often and adding beef broth when necessary.
Bring a large pot of salted water to a boil and cook the pappardelle.
Drain and add to the sauce. Serve hot.

This recipe uses mirepoix, a mix of finely chopped onion, carrot and celery often used as a flavoring base for many soups, sauces and braises.

Preparation time **40 minutes**
Cooking time **1 hour**
Level **medium**
Wine **Chianti Classico**

tagliolini with mixed shellfish

Ingredients for 4 servings
Tagliolini:

1 lb (500 g) mixed shellfish (cockles, clams and mussels)

3 tbsps extra-virgin olive oil

1 garlic clove, minced

1/2 red chili pepper, deseeded and minced

parsley, minced

1 tomato, deseeded and diced

salt

14 oz (400 g) fresh egg tagliolini or spaghetti

Wash the shellfish, debearding the mussels and soaking the clams in cold, salted water for 30 minutes to remove any sand.
Heat the olive oil in a frying pan with the garlic and chili. Add the cockles and cook, covered, over medium heat. After 5 minutes add the clams, and then the mussels, and cook until opened. Sprinkle with parsley and add the tomato. Lightly season with salt.
Bring a large pot of salted water to a boil and cook the tagliolini until al dente.
Drain and toss with the sauce, letting the pasta soak up some of the cooking juices. Serve hot.

Shellfish should be used as fresh as possible, and not overcooked, otherwise it tends to dry out. It is therefore important to add the shellfish which requires the longest cooking time first to the pot, and then the other ones, in order of how fast they cook.

Preparation time **20 minutes**
Cooking time **15 minutes**
Level **easy**
Wine **Trentino Müller Thurgau**

Fresh Pasta

trofie with creamed asparagus

Ingredients for 4 servings

Trofie:

20 asparagus spears
(about 10½ oz or 300 g)

4 tbsps extra-virgin olive oil

2 garlic cloves

salt and pepper

1/2 cup (120 ml) vegetable broth

1/3 cup (80 ml) heavy cream

1 lb (500 g) fresh trofie
or other short pasta

Trim off the woody base of the asparagus and slice
the rest into rounds, leaving a few tips whole for garnish.
Heat the olive oil in a frying pan and sauté the garlic.
Add the asparagus, salt and pepper and cook for
10 minutes, adding a little broth every so often.
When the asparagus is tender, remove the garlic
and the whole tips. Discard the garlic and reserve
the whole tips. Puree the remaining asparagus together
with the cream. Return the sauce in the frying pan.
Bring a large pot of salted water to a boil and cook
the trofie. Drain and transfer to the pan with the sauce.
Sauté for a few minutes then serve hot, garnished
with the asparagus tips.

Preparation time **15 minutes**
Cooking time **20 minutes**
Level **easy**
Wine **Riviera Ligure di Ponente Vermentino**

black tagliolini with marinated salmon

Ingredients for 4 servings

Sauce:

14 oz (400 g) salmon fillet, sliced

juice and julienned zest of 1 organic lime

fresh dill, minced, salt and pepper

4 tbsps extra-virgin olive oil

1/3 cup (80 ml) heavy cream

1 tbsp mustard

Tagliolini:

3 cups plus 3 tbsps (14 oz or 400 g) all-purpose flour

2 oz (60 g) squid ink (nero di seppie)

3 eggs plus 2 egg yolks

Garnish:

salmon roe, dill sprigs

Mustard is an appetite stimulant, and can be used as seeds, powder or a paste. Dijon mustard, also called moutarde, is milder than spicy English mustard.

Place the salmon in a bowl with the lime juice, dill, salt, pepper and 1 tablespoon olive oil.
Refrigerate for 1 hour, stirring every so often.
Mix together all the tagliolini ingredients to form a smooth dough. Roll it out into sheets and cut into tagliolini using a pasta machine. Whisk together the cream, mustard, remaining 3 tablespoons olive oil and julienned lime zest.
Heat a non-stick frying pan and sear the salmon slices for 30 seconds on each side, then set aside and keep warm. Bring a large pot of salted water to a boil and cook the tagliolini until al dente.
Drain, reserving some of the pasta cooking water, and toss with the cream-mustard mixture, adding a little cooking water if it seems too dry.
Serve the pasta topped with the salmon slices, garnished with salmon roe and dill sprigs.

Preparation time **30 minutes**
Cooking time **5 minutes**
Level **medium**
Wine **Bianco d'Alcamo Riserva**

tagliolini and scallops with pinot bianco

Ingredients for 4 servings
Tagliolini:

6 tbsps extra-virgin olive oil

1 tab of butter, **1** shallot, minced

9 oz (250 g) scallops, diced

1/2 cup (120 ml) Pinot Bianco
or other white wine

1 cup (5½ oz or 150 g) asparagus tips

4 small zucchini, julienned

4 squash blossoms, chopped, salt

fresh ginger, grated

14 oz (400 g) fresh egg tagliolini
or other long, thin pasta

Heat the olive oil and sauté half the shallot.
Add the scallops, sauté briefly, then add the wine.
Transfer to a covered container and keep warm.
In the same pan melt the butter and sauté the remaining
shallot. Add the asparagus and zucchini, cover and cook
for 10 minutes, adding a little hot water if necessary.
Just before they are done, add the zucchini flowers.
Add the scallops to the vegetables, season with salt
and add a little grated ginger.
Bring a pot of salted water to a boil and cook the tagliolini,
then toss with the sauce in the frying pan. Serve hot.

To best cook pasta, the water must be
abundant and salted. The rule is 4 cups
(1 litre) of water for every 3 ½ oz
(100 g) of pasta. To avoid sticking,
adding a few spoonfuls of olive oil
to the water before it reaches a boil.

Preparation time **20 minutes**
Cooking time **20 minutes**
Level **easy**
Wine **Alto Adige Pinot Bianco**

parsley passatelli with oyster mushrooms and pumpkin

Ingredients for 4 servings

Passatelli:

2 eggs, salt and pepper, nutmeg

1 cup (2 oz or 50 g) minced parsley

5 tbsps all-purpose flour

1/2 cup (2½ oz or 70 g) breadcrumbs

5 tbsps grated Grana Padano cheese

Sauce:

1¾ cups (7 oz or 200 g) cubed pumpkin or other winter squash

2 tbsps extra-virgin olive oil

2½ cups (7 oz or 200 g) sliced oyster mushrooms

vegetable broth, salt and pepper

Passatelli are a traditional pasta from Romagna, made with a breadcrumb dough. A passatelli-making tool forces the dough through a plate with small holes in it, creating strings which fall directly into boiling water or broth.

Break the eggs into a round-bottomed bowl.
Mix them with a wooden spoon, and while mixing, gradually add the salt, pepper, freshly grated nutmeg, parsley, flour, breadcrumbs and finally the cheese, to obtain a smooth mixture without lumps.
Let rest for 1 hour.
Meanwhile, cook the pumpkin in the vegetable broth in a covered saucepan until tender, then drain and pass through a sieve.
Heat the olive oil in a frying pan and sauté the mushrooms, seasoning them with salt and pepper.
Bring a large pot of salted water to a boil and then drop the passatelli directly into it using a passatelli-making tool or a potato ricer.
Cook them for 3 minutes, then drain.
Arrange the passatelli on plates and serve with the pumpkin puree and the sautéed oyster mushrooms.

Preparation time **20 minutes**
Cooking time **35 minutes**
Level **easy**
Wine **Colli Piacentini Sauvignon**

creamy saffron tagliolini with crispy asparagus

Ingredients for 4 servings

Tagliolini:

2⅓ cups plus 1 tbsp
(10½ oz or 300 g) all-purpose flour

3 eggs

Sauce:

3/4 cup (180 ml) heavy cream

2 pinches of saffron, salt and pepper

2 tbsps extra-virgin olive oil

2 garlic cloves, unpeeled

25 asparagus tips

Mix together the flour and eggs and work vigorously
to obtain a dough, then let rest for 30 minutes.
Roll out very thin sheets using a pasta machine, making
them as thin as possible.
Flour the pasta sheets and roll them up, then slice them
very thinly with a knife to make tagliolini, or cut them
with a pasta machine.
Arrange them on a well-floured clean kitchen towel to dry.
Bring the cream and saffron to a simmer. Season with salt
and pepper and let reduce for a few minutes.
Heat the olive oil with the garlic cloves until very hot
then fry the asparagus tips until crispy.
Bring a large pot of salted water to a boil and cook
the tagliolini until al dente.
Drain and transfer to a pan with the saffron cream
and sauté briefly. Serve, topped with the asparagus tips.

Alternatively the tagliolini
dough can be colored with
saffron. Dissolve a pinch of
saffron in 1 tablespoon warm
water and add it to the dough.

Preparation time **8 minutes**
Cooking time **2 minutes**
Level **easy**
Wine **Bardolino Chiaretto**

chianti tagliolini with sausage

Ingredients for 4 servings

Tagliolini:

3 cups plus 3 tbsps (14 oz or 400 g) all-purpose flour

6 egg yolks

1/2 cup (120 ml) Chianti Classico or other red wine

salt, semolina flour

Sauce:

2 tbsps extra-virgin olive oil

1 garlic clove

6½ oz (180 g) sausage meat

1 tsp fennel seeds, salt and pepper

3 tbsps Chianti Classico wine

Mix the flour, egg yolks, wine and salt to make a smooth, elastic dough. Wrap in plastic wrap and refrigerate for 30 minutes.
Roll the dough out with a pasta machine and then cut it into tagliolini.
Sprinkle the tagliolini with semolina and set aside to dry.
Heat the olive oil with the garlic clove and crumble in the sausage meat. Add the fennel seeds, salt and pepper and brown for 2 minutes, then add the wine.
Bring a large pot of salted water to a boil and cook the tagliolini.
Add a little of the pasta cooking water to the sauce.
Drain the pasta and transfer to the sauce.
Sauté to mix well, then serve hot.

164

A word of advice: When sautéing a delicate pasta like tagliolini or tagliatelle in the pan with the sauce, use two large serving forks to move the pasta around without breaking it.

Preparation time **25 minutes**
Cooking time **10 minutes**
Level **easy**
Wine **Chianti Classico**

black tagliolini with clams

Ingredients for 4 servings
Tagliolini:

1¾ lb (800 g) clams, salt

7 oz (200 g) barba di frate (see note)
or spinach leaves

5 tbsps extra-virgin olive oil

1 red chili pepper, minced

1 garlic clove, minced

1 bunch of parsley, minced

1 spring onion, minced

2 vine-ripened tomatoes

14 oz (400 g) fresh squid-ink tagliolini

Soak the clams in cold salted water for 30 minutes.
Blanch the barba di frate or spinach in boiling salted
water for 5 minutes.
Heat the olive oil in a frying pan and sauté the chile
pepper, garlic and parsley. Add the spring onion and
clams, cover and cook until all the shells are open.
Halve the tomatoes, remove the seeds and dice the flesh.
Take the cover off the pan with the clams and add the
tomatoes and the barba di frate or spinach.
Season with salt and remove from the heat, but keep
covered.
Bring a large pot of salted water to a boil and cook
the tagliolini until al dente. Drain and transfer to the pan
with the sauce. Return to the heat and sauté briefly
to reduce. Serve hot.

Barba di frate, also known as agretti
or saltwort, has long, thin leaves and a
slightly acidic, metallic taste. It typically
grows in coastal regions and is usually
boiled and eaten as a leafy vegetable,
but can also be eaten raw.

Preparation time **20 minutes**
Cooking time **20 minutes**
Level **easy**
Wine **Friuli Collio Sauvignon**

fresh trofie with clams and broccoli rabe

Ingredients for 4 servings

Sauce:

1 lb (500 g) clams

coarse salt

3 tbsps extra-virgin olive oil

2 garlic cloves, 1 minced
and 1 smashed

1 bunch broccoli rabe or turnip tops,
roughly chopped

1/2 dried red chili pepper

parsley, minced

Trofie:

1¾ cups (8 oz or 230 g)
all-purpose flour

salt

To make the clams open faster,
add ½ cup (120 ml) white wine
to the pan with the clams, and
cook them over very high heat.

Wash the clams and place them in a basin with water
and a handful of coarse salt to purge them for 30 minutes.
Mound the flour on a work surface and add a pinch of salt
and enough water to make a firm dough. Break off pieces
the size of a chickpea and roll on a wooden board with
the palm of the hand to make long, twisted shapes, fatter
in the middle and pointed at the ends.
Heat 1 tablespoon olive oil with the minced garlic
and sauté the broccoli rabe for 3 minutes.
Rinse the clams and put them in another frying pan
with the remaining olive oil, smashed garlic and chile.
As soon as they open, transfer to a plate and keep warm.
Remove the garlic and chile from the clam cooking liquid.
Bring a pot of salted water to the boil and cook the trofie.
Drain and toss in the clam cooking liquid.
Add the broccoli rabe, cook for 2 minutes, then add the
clams. Stir well and serve hot, sprinkled with parsley.

Preparation time **10 minutes**
Cooking time **20 minutes**
Level **easy**
Wine **Vermentino della Riviera Ligure di Ponente**

trofie with walnut sauce

Ingredients for 4 servings
Trofie:

2 oz (50 g) fresh bread crumb (no crusts)

3/4 cup (180 ml) milk

3 cups (10½ oz or 300 g) walnuts

salt

1 garlic clove, peeled

5 tbsps Ligurian extra-virgin olive oil

6 tbsps grated Parmesan cheese

14 oz (400 g) fresh trofie or other short pasta

Soak the bread in the milk until soft, then drain and squeeze out excess milk.
Soak the walnuts in hot water for a few minutes, then drain and rub off the skins.
Grind them with a mortar and pestle together with a pinch of salt, the garlic and the soaked bread.
Pass the mixture through a sieve, then dilute it with olive oil and stir in the grated Parmesan cheese.
Bring a large pot of salted water to a boil and cook the trofie. Drain them, reserving some of the pasta cooking water, and toss with the walnut sauce.
Add a little of the cooking water if necessary.
Serve immediately.

Trofie are a typical Ligurian pasta, traditionally eaten with pesto, or, as in the town of Camogli, with "favored" pesto, made with the addition of boiled potatoes and green beans.

Preparation time **20 minutes**
Cooking time **15 minutes**
Level **easy**
Wine **Riviera Ligure di Ponente Pigato**

millefeuille with asparagus and pecorino béchamel

Ingredients for 4 servings

Asparagus:

12 asparagus spears

2 tbsps extra-virgin olive oil

2 garlic cloves, minced

salt and pepper

Béchamel:

4 cups (1 litre) milk

nutmeg, salt

1/4 cup (2 oz or 60 g) butter

1/2 cup (2 oz or 60 g) all-purpose flour

5½ oz (150 g) Pecorino cheese,grated

Pasta:

1 lb (500 g) fresh egg pasta sheets

Trim off the woody end of the asparagus spears and slice the rest into rounds, leaving the tips whole.
Heat the olive oil in a frying pan and sauté the garlic.
Add the asparagus and sauté until tender. Season with salt and pepper.
Bring the milk to a boil with a pinch of freshly grated nutmeg and salt.
In another pan, melt the butter and stir in the flour.
Pour in the boiling milk, whisking constantly, and whisk in the grated Pecorino. Roll the pasta sheets out until very thin, then cut them into equal-sized squares.
Bring a large pot of salted water to a boil and cook the pasta. Drain and lay out on a clean kitchen towel to dry.
Compose plates by layering pasta sheets with the béchamel and asparagus, repeating the layers 3 times, and finishing with a drizzle of olive oil and a sprinkling of freshly grated nutmeg. Serve hot.

The Pecorino in the béchamel can be replaced by Brie.

Preparation time **30 minutes**
Cooking time **20 minutes**
Level **easy**
Wine **Friuli Collio Sauvignon**

filled pasta

Pasta

rabbit canolini with red wine sauce

Ingredients for 4 servings

Filling:

9 oz (250 g) rabbit

3 tbsps extra-virgin olive oil

1/4 cup (1 oz or 30 g) minced celery,
carrot and onion

5 juniper berries, smashed

2 oz (50g) ricotta, salt and pepper

Leek sauce:

1 potato, peeled and diced

2 leeks, sliced, salt

Red wine sauce:

1 bottle (750 ml) Merlot wine

1 medium onion, minced

1 tbsp thyme leaves, cornstarch, salt

Pasta dough:

3 cups plus 3 tbsps (14 oz or 400 g)
all-purpose flour

4 tbsps extra-virgin olive oil, **4** eggs

4 tbsps grated Parmesan cheese, salt

Debone the rabbit and chop the meat. Heat the olive oil in a saucepan and brown the celery, carrot and onion. Add the rabbit and juniper berries, let brown then add some water. Let cook for 30 minutes, then remove from the heat, let cool slightly and chop finely with a knife. Stir in the ricotta and adjust salt and pepper. Boil the potato and leeks in salted water until tender. Drain and puree in a blender or food processor, then pass through a sieve to obtain a sauce. Keep warm. Bring the wine to a boil with the onion and thyme. Cook down to a third of the original volume, then strain. Whisk in a little cornstarch to thicken, then adjust salt to taste. Mix together the flour and eggs to make a smooth dough. Roll it out thinly and cut out circles, half of them 2 inches (5 cm) in diameter, and the other half 1½ inches (4 cm) in diameter. Top the larger circles with some of the rabbit mixture and place a smaller circle on top. Press around the edges to seal, then bri together two opposite sides and pinch firmly to adhere. Bring a large pot of salted water to a boil and cook the canolini. Drain and toss with olive oil and grated Parmesan. Compose plates with a layer of leek sauce, then the canolini, then finish with the red wine sauce. Serve immediately.

Preparation time **1 hour**
Cooking time **1 hour**
Level **medium**
Wine **Friuli Collio Merlot**

Filled Pasta

sturgeon and orange ravioli with taggiasca olive sauce

Ingredients for 4 servings

Pasta dough:

1½ cups plus **1½** tbsps (7 oz or 200 g) all-purpose flour

3/4 cup (3½ oz or 100 g) whole-wheat flour

2 eggs, **1** tbsp water, salt

Filling:

1 potato, **1** garlic clove, **1** tbsp heavy cream

6 tbsps extra-virgin olive oil

5½ oz (150 g) sturgeon fillet, chopped

1/2 cup (120 ml) dry white wine

1 tbsp salted capers, rinsed

grated zest of **1** organic orange

Sauce:

coarse salt, **4** tomatoes, diced

3½ oz (100 g) sturgeon fillet

2 tbsps extra-virgin olive oil

1 garlic clove, minced, parsley, minced

5 tbsps Taggiasca or other black olives, pitted and chopped, salt and pepper

fresh basil, torn into small pieces

Mix together all the pasta dough ingredients to form a smooth dough. Wrap in plastic wrap and refrigerate for 30 minutes. Preheat the oven to 375°F (190°C or Gas Mark 5). Boil the potato until tender, then drain and peel. Heat the olive oil for the filling and sauté the garlic clove. Add the sturgeon and pour over the wine. Cook for 5 minutes, then puree the fish with the cream, boiled potato, capers and orange zest. Pour a layer of coarse salt in a baking dish. Place the sturgeon fillet for the sauce on top and cover with more coarse salt. Bake for 25 minutes. Heat the olive oil for the sauce and sauté the garlic and parsley. Add the tomatoes and olives. Remove the fish from the oven, discard the salt and crumble the fish into the tomato mixture. Adjust salt and pepper. Roll the pasta dough out, not too thinly, into 2 sheets. Cover one of them with spoonfuls of the filling mixture and lay the other one over the top. Press around the filling then cut out ravioli with a ravioli or cookie cutter. Bring a large pot of salted water to a boil and add a drizzle of olive oil. Cook the ravioli for 3 minutes. Drain and transfer to the pan with the sauce. Sprinkle with basil and serve.

Preparation time **40 minutes**
Cooking time **30 minutes**
Level **medium**
Wine **Riviera Ligure di Ponente Pigato**

ricotta, fennel and orange ravioli
with roasted cherry tomatoes

Ingredients for 4 servings

Pasta dough:

2⅓ cups plus 1 tbsp
(10½ oz or 300 g) all-purpose flour

3 eggs, salt

Filling:

1 tbsp extra-virgin olive oil

1/2 white onion, minced

1 small fennel bulb, thinly sliced

1 egg yolk, salt and pepper

1 thyme sprig, leaves only

9 oz (250 g) sheep's milk ricotta

1 tbsp grated Parmesan cheese

grated zest of 1 organic orange

Sauce:

15 ripe cherry tomatoes

2 garlic cloves, smashed

2 tbsps extra-virgin olive oil

basil, minced, salt

Mix together the pasta dough ingredients to form a smooth dough. Wrap in plastic wrap and refrigerate for 30 minutes. Preheat the oven to 400°F (200°C or Gas Mark 6). Heat the olive oil for the filling and sauté the onion, adding a little water to stop it coloring too much. When transparent, add the fennel, salt and pepper and cook for 10 minutes, adding a little water if necessary. Stir in the thyme and let cool.

Puree the fennel mixture in a food processor and stir in the ricotta, egg yolk, Parmesan and orange zest and adjust salt and pepper. Roll the pasta dough out and use the filling to form ravioli in any shape desired. Toss the cherry tomatoes in a bowl with the garlic, olive oil, basil and salt. Transfer to a baking tray and roast in the oven for 20 minutes.

Then either smash the cloves lightly or remove the garlic and puree the tomatoes in a food processor.

Bring a large pot of salted water to a boil and cook the ravioli. Drain and transfer to serving plates. Top with the roast cherry tomatoes and serve.

Preparation time **15 minutes**
Cooking time **10 minutes**
Level **easy**
Wine **Sicilia Chardonnay**

genoa-style ravioli

Ingredients for 6 servings

Filling:

10½ oz (300 g) escarole
1 bread roll, **7** oz (200 g) borage
3 tbsps (1½ oz or 40 g) butter
7 oz (200 g) veal, chopped
2 oz (50 g) sausage, crumbled
3 tbsps grated Parmesan cheese
4 eggs, beaten, salt and pepper, nutmeg

Pasta dough:

4¾ cups (1⅓ lb or 600 g)
all-purpose flour
2 eggs, salt

Sauce:

1/4 cup (2 oz or 60 g) butter
1 rosemary sprig, **1** onion, minced
1/2 celery stalk, minced
5½ oz (300 g) ground beef
3/4 cup (180 ml) red wine
2 cups (500 ml) beef broth
3 tomatoes, diced, salt and pepper
grated Parmesan cheese

Trim off the tough stalks from the escarole and borage and rough chop the leaves. Wash under running water, then without rinsing cook the leaves in a frying pan for 5 minutes. Drain and finely chop. Melt the butter for the filling in a saucepan and brown the veal and sausage meat. Remove from the heat and finely chop the meat. Reserve the cooking juices. Remove the crust from the bread roll. Soak the crumb in the meat cooking juices, then add it to the meat. Stir in the escarole and borage, grated Parmesan and eggs. Season with salt, pepper and a pinch of freshly grated nutmeg. Mix together until thoroughly combined. Mix together the pasta dough ingredients, adding enough water to form a smooth dough. Roll the dough out thinly. Place spoonfuls of the filling on half the dough, then fold over the other half and cut out ravioli using a rolling cutter or a cookie cutter. Dust with flour and set on a tray to dry. Melt the butter in a saucepan. Sauté the onion and celery, then add the beef and brown. Add the rosemary and wine and reduce. Add the tomatoes and beef broth and simmer until the sauce has thickened. Adjust sauce and pepper. Bring a large pot of salted water to a boil and cook the ravioli. Drain and toss with the sauce. Serve hot, sprinkled with grated Parmesan.

Preparation time **50 minutes**
Cooking time **2 hours 20 minutes**
Level **medium**
Wine **Bardolino Chiaretto**

chard tortelli in parmesan cream
with hazelnuts

Ingredients for 4 servings

Pasta dough:

1 cup plus 3 tbsps (5½ oz or 150 g)
all-purpose flour

1 egg plus 1 egg yolk

1/2 tbsp extra-virgin olive oil, salt

Filling:

3 cups (3½ oz or 100 g) chopped
Swiss chard

9 oz (250 g) ricotta

1/2 tbsp grated Parmesan cheese

nutmeg, salt and pepper

Sauce:

3 tbsps grated Parmesan cheese

3 tbsps hot vegetable broth

3-4 tbsps hazelnuts, finely chopped

Mound the flour on a wooden pastry board and make
a well in the center.
Place the egg, egg yolk, olive oil and salt in the well
and mix together quickly to form a smooth dough.
Wrap in plastic wrap and refrigerate for 20 minutes.
Meanwhile blanch the Swiss chard in boiling water.
Drain and puree in a food processor, then stir in the ricotta
and Parmesan. Season with freshly grated nutmeg, salt
and pepper to taste.
Roll the pasta dough out into a thin sheet.
Place spoonfuls of the chard filling around half the dough,
then fold over the other half.
Press around the filling, then use a serrated ravioli
or cookie cutter to cut out square or rectangular tortelli.
Place the grated Parmesan for the sauce in a bowl
and whisk in the hot vegetable broth to form a smooth
cream. Bring a large pot of salted water to a boil and cook
the tortelli. Drain and serve with the Parmesan cream
and hazelnuts.

Preparation time **45 minutes**
Cooking time **5 minutes**
Level **easy**
Wine **Colli di Parma Lambrusco**

guinea hen and foie gras agnolotti with amarone

Ingredients for 4 servings
Pasta dough:

2⅓ cups plus 1 tbsp (10½ oz or 300 g) all-purpose flour
2 eggs plus 2 egg yolks, salt

Filling:

3 tbsps extra-virgin olive oil
1 small white onion, minced
1 carrot, minced, **1** celery stalk, minced
1/2 guinea hen, cut into 4 pieces
3/4 cup (180 ml) Amarone della Valpolicella or other red wine
salt and pepper
1/2 cup (120 ml) hot chicken broth
7 oz (200 g) fresh goose foie gras (or 3½ oz or 100 g cooked, seasoned foie gras), sliced

Mix together the pasta dough ingredients to form a smooth dough. Wrap in plastic wrap and refrigerate for 20 minutes. Heat the olive oil in a saucepan and sauté the onion, carrot and celery. Add the guinea hen and brown for 5 minutes, then add the wine. Season with salt and pepper and cook for another 7-8 minutes, adding hot broth gradually. Remove the guinea hen from the pan, let cool slightly, then debone the meat and chop it finely with a knife. Strain the vegetables from the cooking liquid, reserving the cooking liquid.
Heat a non-stick frying pan and sear the foie gras slices on both sides. Pat dry with paper towels, then dice. Mix together with guinea hen and vegetables.
Roll the pasta dough out thinly. Place many small mounds of the filling on half the dough and then fold over the other half. Cut out agnolotti with a round serrated cookie cutter. Reduce the cooking liquid down to half the original volume. Bring a large pot of salted water to a boil and cook the agnolotti. Drain and drizzle with the reduced cooking liquid. Serve immediately.

Guinea hen, also known as guinea fowl, are native to Africa, but have long been domesticated in Europe. Their flavorful meat is rich in protein and fat, providing high energy and nutrients.

Preparation time **40 minutes**
Cooking time **25 minutes**
Level **medium**
Wine **Amarone della Valpolicella**

Filled Pasta

anolini and tortelli with parmesan

Ingredients for 4 servings
Anolini:

7 oz (200 g) egg pasta dough,
made with yolks only
5 oz (150 g) cooked beef, chopped
2 oz (50 g) prosciutto, chopped
2 cups (500 ml) beef broth

Pumpkin tortelli:

1 tab of butter, **1** tbsp minced onion
1/4 pumpkin or other winter
squash, cubed
vegetable broth, salt and pepper
2 tbsps grated Parmesan cheese
2 amaretti cookies, crumbled
7 oz (200 g) egg pasta dough

Garnish:

grated Parmesan cheese
1 slice of ham, julienned

Sauce:

3/4 cup (200 ml) Lambrusco
or other light red wine
1 shallot, sliced, **1** tsp sugar

Roll out the pasta dough for the anolini and form anolini filled with a mixture of beef and prosciutto.
Melt the butter for the tortelli and sauté the onion, then add the pumpkin. Pour over a little broth and cook for 15 minutes over low heat. Puree the pumpkin and stir in the Parmesan, amaretti, salt and pepper.
Roll out the pasta dough and make tortelli with the pumpkin mixture, cutting them with a serrated rolling cutter. Melt the grated Parmesan in a non-stick pan, turn out onto a cold surface and cut out 4 circles.
Reduce the wine, shallot and sugar in a saucepan over very low heat. Boil the tortelli in salted water and toss them with melted butter.
Boil the anolini in the beef broth. Sauté the ham strips in a frying pan until crunchy. Serve the anolini in a glass with hot broth. Serve the tortelli with the Lambrusco reduction, some grated Parmesan, the Parmesan wafer and the spalla cotta.

Preparation time **45 minutes**
Cooking time **30 minutes**
Level **medium**
Wine **Lambrusco delle Terre Verdiane**

farro cannoncini with porcini mushrooms and marjoram sauce

Ingredients for 4 servings

Pasta dough:

1 cup plus 3 tbsps (5½ oz or 150 g) farro flour

1 cup plus 3 tbsps (5½ oz or 150 g) all-purpose flour

7 egg yolks, salt

Filling:

6½ oz (180 g) lightly smoked ham, chopped

5½ oz (150 g) Ravaggiolo cheese or other fresh, soft cheese

1 egg, beaten, **1** tsp marjoram, salt

Sauce:

1/2 cup (120 ml) milk, **1** garlic clove

1/2 cup (120 ml) heavy cream

2 marjoram sprigs, salt and pepper

1 pinch of cornstarch

2 tbsps extra-virgin olive oil

2 fresh porcini mushrooms, cleaned and chopped

Mix together the ingredients for the pasta dough until smooth. Wrap in plastic wrap and refrigerate for 20 minutes. Mince the ham and cheese together in a food processor, then stir in the egg, marjoram and salt. Bring the milk and cream to a boil with the marjoram then simmer gently over low heat until reduced. Season with salt and pepper and whisk in the cornstarch to thicken. Roll the pasta into thin sheets using a pasta machine. Cut into long strips. Fill a pastry bag with the ham mixture and pipe a stripe of filling down the middle of each strip. Roll the dough up tightly around the filling and brush a little water along the edge to help it stick. Cut the rolls into 1½ inch (4 cm) lengths. Bring a large pot of salted water to a boil and cook the cannoncini. Meanwhile heat the olive oil and garlic clove and sauté the porcini mushrooms. Add the drained cannoncini. Serve together with the creamy marjoram sauce.

Preparation time **40 minutes**
Cooking time **20 minutes**
Level **medium**
Wine **Trentino Nosiola**

pea cappellacci with lobster bisque

Ingredients for 4 servings
Filling:

3¾ cups (1 lb or 500 g) spring peas, salt
4 tbsps extra-virgin olive oil, **1** leek, minced
3½ oz (100 g) prosciutto, in 1 piece
1 bunch of aromatic herbs

Pasta dough:

8 cups (2 lb 3 oz or 1 kg) all-purpose flour
6 eggs plus 8 egg yolks

Bisque:

4 tbsps extra-virgin olive oil
1/2 leek, minced, **2** marjoram sprigs
9 basil leaves, rosemary sprigs
1 pinch dried chili flakes
1 – 1⅓ lb (500-600 g) lobster, shelled
2 cups (500 ml) lobster-shell broth
salt and pepper, chives

Blanch the peas in boiling salted water until tender. Heat the oil for the filling in frying pan and sauté the leek and prosciutto. Add the peas, a little water and the herbs. Let the liquid evaporate, then remove the prosciutto and herbs and puree the peas. Strain the puree. Transfer to a pastry bag. Mix together the pasta dough ingredients to make a smooth dough. Roll out into a thin sheet. Pip mounds of filling on the sheet about 1 inch (2½ cm) apart. Using a rolling cutter cut out squares around the filling, then form the cappellacci by folding the squares into triangles, sealing both edge and then bringing two opposite corners together. Heat 2 tablespoo oil for the bisque in a saucepan. Sauté the leek with the marjoram, 1 rosemary sprig and the chili. Add the lobster claw meat and brov for 1 minute. Add a few ice cubes and 3 basil leaves. Add the lobste shell broth, salt and pepper and cook over low heat for 10 minutes Puree the lobster mixture, stir in 1 tablespoon oil and pass through a sieve. Bring a pot of salted water to a boil and cook the cappellac Drain in a frying pan with oil and a little of the lobster sauce. Slice the rest of the lobster meat, place on a baking tray with rosemary, drizzle with oil and broil for 2 minutes until cooked through. Pour the remaining lobster sauce in bottom of shallow soup bowls and top with pasta and with a medallion of the lobster.

Preparation time **40 minutes**
Cooking time **1 hour**
Level **difficult**
Wine **Terre di Franciacorta Bianco**

burrata and potato cappellacci
with bitter greens

Ingredients for 4 servings

Pasta dough:

1½ cups plus 1½ tbsps (7 oz or 200 g) all-purpose flour

6 tbsps semolina flour, **2** egg whites

2 tbsps extra-virgin olive oil

3/4 cup (180 ml) water

Filling:

1⅔ lb (750 g) potatoes, salt and pepper

1 tbsp extra-virgin olive oil

6 oz (175 g) burrata cheese (see note), chopped

Sauce:

2 tbsps extra-virgin olive oil

1/2 garlic clove, minced

1 rosemary sprig, leaves only, salt

2 lb (1 kg) bitter greens (turnip tops or broccoli rabe)

Burrata is a fresh cheese from Puglia made of an outer shell of mozzarella filled with a mixture of mozzarella scraps and cream.

Mix the pasta dough ingredients together to form a smooth dough. Wrap in plastic wrap and refrigerate. Boil the potatoes until tender, then drain, peel and mash with a potato masher or in a potato ricer. Season with salt and pepper and stir in a drizzle of olive oil. Stir in the burrata.

Roll out the dough into a very thin sheet. Pipe small mounds of the filling on the sheet about 1 inch (2½ cm) apart. Using a rolling cutter cut out squares around the filling, then form the cappellacci by folding the squares into triangles, sealing both edges, and then bringing two opposite corners together.

Heat the olive oil for the sauce and sauté the garlic with the rosemary until golden.

Blanch the bitter greens in boiling salted water until tender, then drain and immerse in ice water.

Once cool, drain and puree with the olive oil, garlic and rosemary in a food processor. Bring a large pot of salted water to a boil and cook the cappellacci. Drain and toss with the sauce. Serve drizzled with olive oil.

Preparation time **35 minutes**

Cooking time **40 minutes**

Level **medium**

Wine Friuli **Collio Sauvignon**

194

giant walnut cappellacci
with chanterelles

Ingredients for 4 servings

Pasta dough:

1½ cups plus 1½ tbsps
(7 oz or 200 g) all-purpose flour

2 egg yolks, salt, 1 egg, beaten

Filling:

1¼ cups (4 oz or 120 g) walnuts

2 tbsps sesame oil

6 oz (180 g) ricotta, 1 tbsp mascarpone

1 tbsp grated Parmesan cheese

salt and white pepper

Sauce:

3 cups (10½ oz or 300 g)
chanterelle mushrooms

4 tbsps extra-virgin olive oil

1/2 red chili pepper, minced

1 garlic clove, unpeeled and halved

fresh mint, minced, salt

1 tab of butter

Mix a smooth dough with the flour, egg yolks and salt.
Wrap in plastic wrap and refrigerate.
Toast the walnuts in a frying pan with the sesame oil
and mince them in a food processor.
Mix the walnuts with the ricotta, mascarpone and
Parmesan and season with salt and pepper to taste.
Roll out the dough, not too thinly, and cut out 8 circles
with a diameter of 3 inches (8 cm).
Brush the borders of 4 circles with the beaten egg
and divide the ricotta and walnut mixture between them.
Lay the other circles on top, press around the edges
to seal and trim with a serrated rolling cutter.
Wash the chanterelles and soak in cold water
for 5 minutes. Trim off the base of the stem and quarter
the mushrooms. Heat the olive oil in a frying pan
with the chile and the garlic. Sauté the mushrooms
and mint for 5 minutes over medium heat and season
with salt. Bring a large pot of salted water to the boil
and cook the cappellacci. Drain, toss with the mushrooms
and a pat of butter, and serve.

Preparation time **30 minutes**
Cooking time **15 minutes**
Level **medium**
Wine **Alto Adige Pinot Bianco**

radicchio and ricotta caramelle
with poppy seeds

Ingredients for 4 servings
Pasta dough:

1½ cups plus 1½ tbsps (7 oz or 200 g) all-purpose flour

2/3 cup (4 oz or 120 g) semolina flour

1/2 cup (120 ml) water

2 tbsps extra-virgin olive oil, salt

Filling:

1 pat of butter

1 1/3 lb (600 g) radicchio, preferably Treviso, shredded

salt and pepper, **9** oz (250 g) ricotta

3 tbsps grated Parmesan cheese

Sauce:

3 tbsps hazelnut oil, **1** leek, thinly sliced

3 tbsps extra-virgin olive oil

2½ tbsps poppy seeds, salt

2 tbsps grated Parmesan cheese

Mix the pasta dough ingredients together to form a smooth dough. Wrap in plastic wrap and refrigerate for 20 minutes.
Melt the butter for the filling and sauté the radicchio with a pinch of salt until all liquid has evaporated. Let cool, finely chop and mix with the ricotta. Stir in the Parmesan and adjust salt and pepper. Roll the pasta dough out into thin sheets. Cut into wide strips. Place spoonfuls of the radicchio mixture about 2 inches (5 cm) apart along one side of the strips, then fold them over. Press around the filling with the fingers then cut out rectangular ravioli using a ravioli or cookie cutter. Twist the two ends of each piece as though it was a candy wrapper, pulling the pasta out slightly so it does not get too thick where it is twisted.
Heat the hazelnut oil and olive oil together. Sauté the leek until tender, then add the poppy seeds and salt.
Bring a large pot of salted water to a boil and cook the caramelle. Drain and toss with the poppy sauce. Serve, sprinkled with Parmesan.

Preparation time **45 minutes**
Cooking time **20 minutes**
Level **medium**
Wine **Alto Adige Santa Maddalena**

cuttlefish caramelle with zucchini

Ingredients for 4 servings
Pasta dough:

2 cups (9 oz or 250 g) all-purpose flour
3 tbsps extra-virgin olive oil
2 eggs plus 1 egg yolk
1 pinch of saffron , thyme leaves, salt

Filling:

2 slices of sandwich bread
1/2 cup (120 ml) milk, **1** garlic clove
3 tbsps extra-virgin olive oil
3 cuttlefish, roughly chopped
salt and pepper

Sauce:

1/2 cup (120 ml) white wine
1/2 cup (120 ml) fish broth
1 tab of butter
2 zucchini, deseeded and julienned

Mix together the pasta dough ingredients to obtain a smooth dough. Wrap in plastic wrap and refrigerate for 20 minutes.
Soak the bread in the milk until soft, then drain and squeeze out excess milk. Meanwhile heat the olive oil in a frying pan with the garlic clove. Add the cuttlefish and sauté for 3 minutes.
Remove and discard the garlic. Add the soaked bread and puree in a food processor, adjust the salt and pepper then set aside. Using the same frying pan, heat the wine and fish broth and cook down to reduce over low heat until half the original volume. Roll out the dough into a thin sheet. Cut out rectangles and place a spoonful of the cuttlefish mixture in the center. Fold the rectangle in half and twist the ends so they look like wrapped candies.
Melt the butter in a frying pan, sauté the zucchini for a few minutes, then add the wine and broth reduction.
Bring a pot of salted water to a boil and cook the caramelle for 4 minutes. Toss with the sauce and serve hot.

Preparation time **40 minutes**
Cooking time **15 minutes**
Level **medium**
Wine **Malvasia Istriana**

saffron shrimp parcels

Ingredients for 4 servings

Pasta dough:

2 cups (9 oz or 250 g) all-purpose flour

2 eggs plus **1** egg yolk, **1** pinch of saffron

3 tbsps extra-virgin olive oil, salt

Filling:

10 shrimp, **6** langoustines

2 tbsps extra-virgin olive oil

1 shallot, minced, **1** tbsp breadcrumbs

1 tbsp heavy cream

Sauce:

2 tbsps extra-virgin olive oil

1 carrot, diced

1 onion, diced

1 celery stalk, diced

3/4 cup (7 oz or 200 g) cooked beans

Sauce:

2 tbsps extra-virgin olive oil

1 carrot, **1** onion, **1** celery stalk chopped

Mix together the dough ingredients until smooth, then wrap in plastic wrap and let rest for 20 minutes. Shell the shrimp and langoustines, reserving the shells. Heat the olive oil for the broth and sauté the shells with the carrot, onion and celery, then cover with water and let simmer to obtain a flavorful broth. Strain the broth. Heat the olive oil for the filling and sauté the shallot. Add the shelled shrimp and langoustines. Sauté for 5 minutes, then remove from heat. Set aside a few shrimp and langoustines for garnish. Transfer the remainder to a food processor, add the cream and breadcrumbs and puree. Heat the olive oil for the sauce and sauté the carrot, onion and celery. Add the beans, cover with the shrimp broth and cook for 20 minutes. Roll the dough out thinly, cut into squares and place small piles of the pureed shrimp mixture in the center of each one. Pull the corners of the squares into the middle and pinch tightly closed using the fingertips. Bring a large pot of salted water to a boil. Turn the heat down, add the parcels and simmer until cooked through. Meanwhile puree the cooked beans and serve the parcels over the bean puree, garnished with the reserved shrimp and langoustines.

Preparation time **50 minutes**
Cooking time **35 minutes**
Level **difficult**
Wine **Gambellara**

chicory parcels with char

Ingredients for 4 servings
Dough:

1½ cups plus 1½ tbsps (7 oz or 200 g) all-purpose flour

2 tbsps extra-virgin olive oil, **2** eggs, salt

Filling:

salt and pepper

5½ oz (150 g) chicory

2 tbsps grated Parmesan cheese

2 tbsps extra-virgin olive oil

nutmeg, grated

Sauce:

1/2 cup (120 ml) extra-virgin olive oil

1 large shallot, minced

1/2 red chile pepper, minced

6½ oz (180 g) Atlantic char fillet, deboned and diced

1/2 cup (120 ml) white wine

salt and pepper, parsley, minced

1 pat of butter

Mix together the dough ingredients until smooth, wrap in plastic wrap and let rest for 30 minutes.
Bring a pot of salted water to a boil and cook the chicory until tender. Drain, squeeze out excess water and chop. Mix together the chicory, Parmesan, olive oil, nutmeg, salt and pepper and let cool.
Roll out the dough and cut out circles using a fluted cookie cutter or a glass.
Place 1 teaspoon of the chicory mixture in the center of each circle and close like a little parcel, pinching tightly with the fingers to seal the dough. Set aside.
Heat the olive oil for the sauce in a frying pan and sauté the shallot and chile. Add the char, sauté briefly, then add the white wine. Season with salt, pepper and parsley and continue cooking until cooked through.
Bring a large pot of salted water to a boil and cook the parcels for 3-4 minutes.
Drain, place in bowls or a serving dish and top with the char sauce, adding the butter and pepper.
Serve immediately.

Preparation time **30 minutes**
Cooking time **10 minutes**
Level **medium**
Wine **Etna Bianco**

squab parcels with port and foie gras sauce

Ingredients for 4 servings

Dough:

2 cups (9 oz or 250 g) all-purpose flour

5 egg yolks, salt

Filling:

1 medium potato, salt and pepper

1 tbsp raisins

1 tbsp Vin Santo or other dessert wine

1 squab

3 tbsps extra-virgin olive oil

5 tbsps minced celery, carrot and onion

1/2 cup (120 ml) red wine

Sauce:

2 medium fennel bulbs, cut into wedges

1½ oz (40 g) foie gras

1 tbsp white Port

1/2 cup (120 ml) hot vegetable broth

salt

1 pat of butter, melted

Mix together the flour, egg yolks and salt to form a dough, then wrap in plastic wrap and let rest.
Boil the potato in salted water until tender, then drain, peel and mash. Soak the raisins in Vin Santo.
Clean the squab and season with salt and pepper.
Heat the olive oil and sauté the minced celery, carrot and onion. Add the squab and brown. Add the raisins and Vin Santo. Add the red wine and cook for 12-13 minutes. Remove the squab from the pan and debone.
Return the meat to the pan and add the potato.
Season with salt and pepper. Roll out the pasta dough and cut into 1 inch (2½ cm) squares. Fill with small quantities of the squab mixture and close like little parcels. Steam the fennel. When tender, let cool and chop. Heat a copper frying pan until very hot, then sear the foie gras. Deglaze with Port and hot vegetable broth, then puree the mixture until smooth and add salt to taste.
Bring a large pot of salted water to a boil and cook the parcels. Drain, toss with the butter and serve over chopped fennel with the foie gras sauce.

Preparation time **40 minutes**
Cooking time **50 minutes**
Level **medium**
Wine **Dolcetto di Monferrato**

lobster and skate ravioli over truffled broccoli puree

Ingredients for 4 servings

Dough:

2 cups (9 oz or 250 g) semolina flour

2 cups (9 oz or 250 g) all-purpose flour

5 eggs, extra-virgin olive oil

Filling:

1 skate wing, vegetable broth

1/2 lobster

3½ oz (100 g) sheep's milk ricotta

2 basil leaves, minced

salt and pepper, extra-virgin olive oil

Broccoli:

salt and pepper

3 cups (10½ oz or 300 g) chopped broccoli

4 tbsps extra-virgin olive oil

1 shallot, sliced, **1** garlic clove, minced

chile pepper flakes, **9** oz (250 g) clams

1/2 cup (120 ml) white wine

1 fresh black, shaved

Mix together the dough ingredients until smooth, the wrap in plastic wrap and refrigerate for 2 hours. Poach the skate wing in boiling vegetable broth, then drain and dice. Bring a pot of salted water to a boil and cook the lobster for 4 minutes. Drain and shell the lobster and dice the meat. Mix together the skate, lobster meat, ricotta, basil, salt and pepper with enough olive oil to make a smooth mixture. Bring a pot of salted water to a boil and cook the broccoli until tender. Drain. Heat 2 tablespoons olive oil in a frying pan and sauté the shallot. Add the broccoli and sauté. Heat 2 tablespoons olive oil in another frying pan and sauté the garlic and a pinch of chile pepper flakes. Add the clams and the white wine, cover and cook until the clams have opened. Strain the cooking liquid and set aside. Add half the truffle shavings and the clam cooking liquid to the broccoli. Let cool and the puree the mixture. Roll out the dough and prepare the ravioli with the skate and lobster filling. Bring a large pot of salted water to a boil and cook the ravioli. Drain and serve over the broccoli, garnished with truffle shavings.

Preparation time **15 minutes**
Cooking time **30 minutes**
Level **medium**
Wine **Ischia Bianco**

cabbage and speck parcels

Ingredients for 4 servings

Dough:

2 cups (9 oz or 250 g) all-purpose flour

2 cups (9 oz or 250 g) buckwheat flour

2 eggs, salt

Filling:

1/2 small head of Savoy cabbage, sliced

1 pat of butter, **1/2** onion, diced

3½ oz (100 g) speck, diced

1 tbsp all-purpose flour

1/2 cup (120 ml) heavy cream

1 tbsp grated Parmesan cheese

salt and pepper, nutmeg, grated

Sauce:

3½ tbsps (2 oz or 50 g) butter, at room temperature

mixed herbs (marjoram, thyme, sage and parsley), minced

2 tbsps grated Parmesan cheese

Mix together the dough ingredients, adding water if necessary, until they form a smooth dough. Let rest for 1 hour. Blanch the Savoy cabbage in boiling water, then drain. Melt the butter in a large frying pan and sauté the onion. Add the speck and cabbage, sprinkle over the flour, add the cream and Parmesan and season with salt, pepper and nutmeg.

Roll the dough out with a pasta machine and cut into small squares. Place a walnut-sized amount of filling in the center of each square and bring in the corners to close like a little parcel. Pinch tightly with the fingers to close.

Mix together the butter for the sauce with the herbs, then melt in a frying pan.

Bring a large pot of salted water to a boil and cook the parcels.

Drain and toss in the pan with the herb butter.

Sprinkle with Parmesan before serving.

Preparation time **40 minutes**
Cooking time **20 minutes**
Level **medium**
Wine **Alto Adige Santa Maddalena**

tuna and vegetable rolls

Ingredients for 4 servings

Dough:

10 spinach leaves

1¼ cups (5½ oz or 160 g) all-purpose flour

6 egg yolks

2 tbsps (1 oz or 30 g) butter, softened

Filling:

1 egg

3 tbsps extra-virgin olive oil

1 shallot, sliced, **1** carrot, diced

1 celery stalk, diced

1/2 cup (120 ml) vegetable broth

1 large zucchini, inner white part discarded, diced

2 tomatoes, deseeded, diced and drained

salt and pepper

6½ oz (180 g) tuna in oil, drained and crumbled

Blanch the spinach then drain, reserving the cooking liquid. Finely chop the spinach.
Mix together the flour, egg yolks, butter, spinach and spinach cooking liquid to make a dough.
Wrap in plastic wrap and let rest for 20 minutes.
Hard-boil the egg, peel and separate the yolk and white. Discard the white.
Heat the olive oil in a large frying pan and sauté the shallot. Add the carrot, celery and vegetable broth and cook for 5 minutes. Add the zucchini and tomatoes, season with salt and pepper and cook for another 2 minutes. Set aside a third of the vegetable mixture and stir the crumbled tuna into the remaining two-thirds. Crumble the hard-boiled egg yolk into the other third. Roll the dough out thinly, then cut into squares.
Bring a large pot of salted water to a boil and cook the squares. Drain. Use the vegetables with the tuna to fill the squares, rolling them up as though they were crêpes,m and season with pepper. Reheat the vegetables with egg yolk and serve as a sauce with the rolls.

Preparation time **25 minutes**
Cooking time **15 minutes**
Level **easy**
Wine **Trentino Nosiola**

savoy cabbage ravioli
with truffle cream

Ingredients for 4 servings

Dough:

1⅔ cups (7 oz or 200 g) all-purpose flour

6 egg yolks, salt

Filling:

2 garlic cloves

4 tbsps extra-virgin olive oil

3 oz (80 g) guanciale or pancetta, thinly sliced and diced

1/4 head Savoy cabbage, julienned

5½ oz (150 g) ricotta, sieved

nutmeg, salt and pepper

Sauce:

1 medium potato, peeled

2 tbsps whipping cream

vegetable broth

1 white truffle, shaved

1 black truffle, shaved

extra-virgin olive oil, salt

Mix together all of the ingredients for the dough and knead until smooth. Roll into a ball and cover with plastic wrap. Let rest. Peel the garlic cloves and remove the inner green shoot. Heat the olive oil in a large frying pan, add the garlic cloves and guanciale and let render. Add the cabbage and cook over high heat. Season to taste with salt and pepper and remove from heat. Add the ricotta and a grating of nutmeg. Using a pasta machine or rolling pin, roll out the dough into a thin sheet. Place teaspoonsfuls of the cabbage filling around half the dough sheet. Brush around the filling piles with water and fold the dough sheet over to cover the filling. Cut out the ravioli using a round cookie cutter, then wrap each one around the index finger and pinch closed. Slice the potato very thinly with a mandolin and cook until tender in a little hot vegetable broth and olive oil. Add the truffle shavings and puree the mixture using an immersion blender. Add the cream and season to taste with salt. Spoon the truffle cream into serving bowls. Boil the ravioli in salted water for 2 minutes. Drain and place the ravioli over the truffle cream. Serve immediately.

Preparation time **35 minutes**
Cooking time **15 minutes**
Level **medium**
Wine **Trentino Marzemino**

lobster and onion ravioli
with shrimp butter

Ingredients for 4 servings
Dough:

2½ cups plus 1 tbsp (11½ oz or 320 g)
all-purpose flour

6 egg yolks, **1** egg, salt

Filling:

1 lobster, poached in court bouillon

1 white onion, thinly sliced

2 tbsps (1 oz or 30 g) butter

7 tbsps fish broth, salt and pepper

Sauce:

4 tbsps (2 oz or 60 g) salted butter,
at room temperature

3½ oz (100 g) shelled and deveined
shrimp, finely chopped

thyme, minced, white pepper

1 small porcini mushroom,
cleaned and thinly sliced

Mix together the ingredients for the dough until smooth and roll into a ball. Cover with plastic wrap and refrigerate until ready to use. Shell the lobster and set the meat aside. Gently sauté the onions in the butter for 30 minutes, adding a little fish broth from time to time. When the onion is transparent, drain off any excess cooking liquid, and dice together with the lobster meat. Season with pinches of salt and pepper. Roll out the pasta dough into two thin sheets. Place teaspoonfuls of the lobster filling around one sheet of dough and cover with a second sheet of dough. Press down around the filling to seal and cut out ravioli using a cookie cutter or rolling pasta cutter. Cover the ravioli with a kitchen towel and set aside. Mix together the butter, shrimp and thyme and season with a pinch of white pepper. Spread the butter mixture into a thin layer on a sheet of parchment paper, roll up and refrigerate. Bring a large pot of salted water to a boil and cook the ravioli for a few minutes. Meanwhile melt the shrimp butter in a large frying pan. Using a slotted spoon, transfer the ravioli into the pan with the butter. Sauté briefly. Serve the ravioli with topped with the thinly sliced porcini mushroom.

Preparation time **40 minutes**
Cooking time **35 minutes**
Level **medium**
Wine **Metodo Classico Franciacorta Dosaggio Zero**

beet ravioli with butter and poppy seeds

Ingredients for 4 servings

Dough:

4 cups (1 lb or 500 g) all-purpose flour

5 eggs, salt

Filling:

1 lb (500 g) red beets

3 tbsps grated Parmesan cheese

1 egg, salt and pepper

Sauce:

7 tbsps (3½ oz or 100 g) butter

2 tbsps breadcrumbs

1 tbps poppy seeds

1 tbsp grated Parmesan cheese

Beets have been considered an aprodisiac since Roman times. They contain boron, a mineral which plays an important role in the production of human sex hormones.

Mix togther the ingredients for the dough and knead to form a smooth dough. Cover in plastic wrap and let rest in the refrigerator until ready to use.
Blanch the beets in boiling salted water until tender. Peel, dice and puree. Stir in the Parmesan and egg and season to taste with salt and pepper. Mix well and set aside. Using a pasta machine or a rolling pin, roll out the pasta dough into thin sheets. Cut out rounds using a cookie cutter and place one teaspoonful of filling in the center of each round. Fold the rounds in half to form a half-moon shape and press down around the edges to seal. Bring a large pot of salted water to a boil and cook the ravioli for about 2 minutes. Meanwhile, melt the butter in a large frying pan. Using a slotted spoon, transfer the cooked ravioli to the pan with the melted butter. Sprinkle over the breadcrumbs and sauté briefly.
Serve the ravioli hot, sprinkled with the poppy seeds and Parmesan.

Preparation time **40 minutes**
Cooking time **30 minutes**
Level **medium**
Wine **Alto Adige Sylvaner**

burrata ravioli with bell pepper and zucchini sauce

Ingredients for 4 servings

Dough:

2⅓ cups plus 1 tbsp (10½ oz or 300 g) all-purpose flour

2 tbsps semolina flour, 2 eggs

2 egg yolks, salt

Filling:

1 whole burrata cheese

thyme leaves, salt and pepper

Sauce:

1 shallot, minced

6 tbsps extra-virgin olive oil

1/3 red bell pepper, diced

1/3 yellow bell pepper, diced

2 zucchini, green part only, julienned

Burrata is a very soft cheese made from mozzarella and cream. Burrata should be purchased as fresh as possible and stored in the coldest part of the refrigerator.

Mix together all of the ingredients for the pasta to form a smooth dough.

Cover with plastic wrap and refrigerate for 20 minutes. Puree the burrata with the thyme leaves in a food processor or blender and season to taste with salt and pepper. Using a pasta machine or a rolling pin, roll out the pasta dough into thin rectangular sheets.

Place teaspoonfuls of the burrata filling along one side of the pasta at 1½ inch (4 cm) intervals.

Fold the dough in half lengthwise, to cover the filling, and press down between each mound of filling to seal. Cut between the filling mounds to form ravioli.

In a large frying pan, sauté the shallot in the olive oil. Add the peppers and cook for 5 minutes over low heat. Add the julienned zucchini and season to taste with salt. Add 2 tablespoons of water and let evaporate.

Bring a large pot of salted water to a boil and cook the ravioli for 2 minutes. Using a slotted spoon, transfer the ravioli into the pan with the sauce. Sauté briefly and serve.

Preparation time **40 minutes**
Cooking time **10 minutes**
Level **medium**
Wine **Trentino Nosiola**

burrata ravioli with broccoli and artichoke sauce

Ingredients for 4 servings

Dough:

1²⁄₃ cups (7 oz or 200 g) all-purpose flour

4 egg yolks, **1** egg

1 tbsp extra-virgin olive oil, salt

Sauce:

1 head broccoli, cut into florets

salt and pepper, **4** medium artichokes

3 tbsps extra-virgin olive oil

1 shallot, minced

1 yellow-fleshed potato, peeled and thinly sliced

2 cups (500 ml) vegetable broth

2 tbsps (1 oz or 20 g) butter

Filling:

1½ lb (250 g) burrata cheese, pureed

Mix together the ingredients for the dough until smooth. Cover with plastic wrap and let rest for 20 minutes. Blanch the broccoli florets in boiling salted water for a few minutes. Drain and transfer to a bowl of ice water until cool, then drain. Trim the tough outer leaves from the artichokes, scoop out the choke and thinly slice the artichoke hearts. Heat the olive oil in a frying pan and add the shallot. Let it soften and add the potatoes and artichokes. Sauté for a few minutes and then cover with hot broth and let cook for 15 minutes. Season to taste with salt and pepper. Roll out the dough into two thin sheets using a pasta machine. Place teaspoonfuls of the burrata filling around the pasta. Cover with the second sheet of pasta and press down around the filling to seal. Cut out the ravioli using a cookie cutter. Puree the artichoke and potato mixture and then pass it through a chinois sieve. Spoon the puree into serving bowls and set aside. Bring a pot of salted water to a boil and cook the ravioli for 2 minutes. Meanwhile melt the butter in a large frying pan and add the broccoli florets. Using a slotted spoon transfer the ravioli to the frying pan and sauté for 1 minute with the broccoli. Place the ravioli and broccoli over the artichoke puree and drizzle with olive oil.

Preparation time **35 minutes**
Cooking time **20 minutes**
Level **medium**
Wine **Etna Bianco**

A chinois is a fine-meshed conical strainer. Take care when using a chinois as it is very delicate.

pansoti with walnut sauce

Ingredients for 6 servings

Pasta dough:

4 cups (1 lb or 500 g) all-purpose flour

3 eggs, salt, white wine

extra-virgin olive oil

Filling:

10½ oz (300 g) Swiss chard
and borage

3 eggs

6 tbsps grated pecorino cheese

3½ oz (100 g) quagliata or other fresh,
soft cheese, salt

Sauce:

5 tbsps walnut sauce
(see recipe on p. 170)

grated Parmesan cheese (optional)

Mound the flour on a work surface and mix in the eggs and a pinch of salt. Work well, adding as much white wine as necessary to create a smooth and uniform dough.
Form into a ball, cover with plastic wrap and set aside.
Boil the Swiss chard and borage until tender.
Drain, squeeze out excess water and chop finely.
Beat the eggs for the filling and mix with the chard, borage, cheeses and salt.
Roll the dough out thinly and cut out 4-inch (10 cm) squares. Place 1 tablespoon of filling in the center of every piece then fold from corner to corner to create a triangle and press the edges to seal.
Arrange the pansoti on a floured tray and let dry.
Bring a large pot of salted water to the boil and cook the pansoti, adding a drizzle of oil to the water so they don't stick. Drain and serve with the walnut sauce and grated Parmesan if desired.

Preparation time **40 minutes**
Cooking time **20 minutes**
Level **medium**
Wine **Rossese di Dolceacqua**

broccoli ravioli
with pine nuts and rosemary

Ingredients for 4 servings

Pasta dough:

2 cups (9 oz or 250 g) all-purpose flour

1/2 cup plus 1½ tbsps (3½ oz or 100 g) very finely ground cornmeal

1 tbsp extra-virgin olive oil

3 eggs, salt, freshly grated nutmeg

Filling:

1 lb (500 g) broccoli, cut into florets, salt

3 tbsps extra-virgin olive oil

2 garlic cloves, minced

1 red chili pepper, minced

3 tbsps grated Parmesan cheese

Sauce:

2½ tbsps pine nuts

2 tbsps extra-virgin olive oil

1 rosemary sprig, leaves only

Mix the pasta dough ingredients together to form a smooth dough.
Wrap in plastic wrap and refrigerate for 20 minutes.
Cook the broccoli in boiling salted water until tender, then drain and let cool. Finely chop and place in a bowl.
Heat the olive oil and sauté the garlic and chile until soft. Strain the oil and add it to the broccoli.
Stir in the Parmesan and a pinch of salt.
Roll out the pasta dough into a thin sheet.
Place small piles of the broccoli mixture on half the sheet, then fold over the other sheet and cut out ravioli with a cookie or ravioli cutter.
Toast the pine nuts in a non-stick frying pan, then grind with a mortar and pestle.
Heat the olive oil for the sauce and sauté the ground pine nuts and rosemary leaves.
Bring a large pot of salted water to a boil and cook the ravioli. Drain and toss with the pine nut mixture.
Serve immediately.

Preparation time **45 minutes**
Cooking time **20 minutes**
Level **medium**
Wine **Alto Adige Pinot Nero**

shrimp and potato ravioli
with pea sauce

Ingredients for 4 servings

Filling:

3 potatoes

8 shrimp

salt and pepper

parsley, minced

Pasta dough:

1½ cups plus 1½ tbsps (7 oz or 200 g) all-purpose flour

7 tbsps milk

Sauce:

1 tbsp extra-virgin olive oil

1 large celery stalk, minced

1 small carrot, minced

1 shallot, minced

1/2 cup (120 ml) white wine

1 cup (4½ oz or 130 g) fresh peas

Boil the potatoes until tender, then drain, peel and mash. Shell the shrimp, reserving the heads and shells. Blanch the shelled shrimp in boiling water for 2 minutes. Mix the pasta dough ingredients together to form a smooth dough. Wrap in plastic wrap and refrigerate for at least 20 minutes. Chop the shrimp and mix into the mashed potatoes. Season with salt and pepper, stir in the parsley, and let sit for at least 10 minutes. Heat the olive oil in a saucepan and sauté the celery, carrot and shallot. Add the shrimp heads and shells, let brown then add the wine. Let reduce, then cover with warm water and continue cooking for 20 minutes. Roll out the pasta dough into a thin sheet. Place small piles of the shrimp-potato mixture on half the sheet, then fold over the other sheet and cut out ravioli with a ravioli or cookie cutter. Pass the shrimp broth through a food mill or strain it with a sieve, then cook down until reduced in volume. Add the peas and cook for 10 minutes. Puree the mixture and adjust salt and pepper. Bring a large pot of salted water to a boil and cook the ravioli. Drain and serve with the pea sauce.

Preparation time **45 minutes**
Cooking time **30 minutes**
Level **medium**
Wine **Friuli Annia Chardonnay**

crab and potato ravioli with chanterelles

Ingredients for 4 servings
Filling:
2 medium potatoes, parsley, minced
5½ oz (150 g) crab meat
2 tbsps extra-virgin olive oil
salt and white pepper
Pasta dough:
2⅓ cups plus 1 tbsp (10½ oz
or 300 g) all-purpose flour
2 eggs plus 2 egg yolks, salt
Sauce:
2 tbsps extra-virgin olive oil
2 garlic cloves, smashed
2½ cups (7 oz or 200 g)
chanterelle mushrooms
3 thyme sprigs, leaves only

Place the potatoes in a saucepan and cover with cold water. Salt and bring to a boil. Cook until tender. Meanwhile, mix the pasta dough ingredients together to form a smooth dough.
Wrap in plastic wrap and refrigerate for 30 minutes.
Drain the potatoes, peel and mash them. Stir in the crab meat, parsley, olive oil, salt and white pepper.
Lightly knead the dough, then roll it out into a thin sheet. Place small piles of the crab-potato mixture on half the sheet, then fold over the other sheet and cut out ravioli using a fluted rolling cutter.
Bring a large pot of salted water to a boil and cook the ravioli. Meanwhile heat the olive oil for the sauce with the garlic cloves and sauté the mushrooms. Deglaze the pan with a little of the ravioli cooking water, and add the thyme. Drain the ravioli and toss in the frying pan with the mushrooms. Serve immediately.

Chanterelles (Cantharellus cibarius) are one of the tastiest wild mushrooms, with a meaty texture and peppery flavor. They grow commonly in chestnut and oak forests.

Preparation time **40 minutes**
Cooking time **20 minutes**
Level **easy**
Wine **Trentino Nosiola**

eggplant and ricotta ravioli with marinated tomatoes

Ingredients for 4 servings

Sauce:

1 mint sprig, leaves only

1 thyme sprig, leaves only, **5** basil leaves

4 tbsps extra-virgin olive oil

1 garlic clove, minced

1 red chili pepper, minced

1½ cups (7 oz or 200 g) cherry tomatoes

3 tbsps grated Parmesan cheese

Pasta dough:

2⅓ cups plus 1 tbsp (10½ oz or 300 g) all-purpose flour

3 eggs

Filling:

3 tbsps extra-virgin olive oil

1 garlic clove, **9** oz (250 g) ricotta

2 eggplants, peeled and diced

5 tbsps grated Parmesan cheese

4 basil leaves, julienned, salt and pepper

Place the mint, thyme and basil for the sauce in a bowl. Heat the olive oil and sauté the garlic and chile. Pour over the herbs and let sit for 30 minutes. Meanwhile, mix the pasta dough ingredients together to form a smooth dough. Wrap in plastic wrap and refrigerate for 20 minutes. Heat the olive oil for the filling with the garlic and sauté the eggplant until tender. Remove from the heat, let cool, then mix together with the ricotta, Parmesan, salt, pepper and basil. Roll out the pasta dough into a thin sheet. Place small piles of the eggplant-ricotta mixture on half the sheet, then fold over the other sheet and cut out ravioli using a ravioli or cookie cutter. Blanch the cherry tomatoes in boiling water for a few seconds, then drain, peel and halve. Place in a colander and let drain. Strain the herb oil, reserving the herbs, and heat the oil in a frying pan. Sauté the cherry tomatoes. Bring a large pot of salted water to a boil and cook the ravioli. Drain and toss with the cherry tomatoes, herbs and remaining Parmesan.

Preparation time **40 minutes**
Cooking time **5 minutes**
Level **medium**
Wine **Falerno del Massico Bianco**

potato ravioli with baby octopus ragù

Ingredients for 4 servings

Pasta dough:

1½ cups plus 1½ tbsps
(7 oz or 200 g) all-purpose flour

3 egg yolks

1 tbsp extra-virgin olive oil, salt

Filling:

1 tab of butter, **1** shallot, minced

2 medium potatoes, peeled
and thinly sliced

1/2 cup (120 ml) vegetable broth

1 thyme sprig, leaves only

Sauce:

2 tomatoes, **3** tbsps extra-virgin olive oil

2 garlic cloves, smashed

1/2 red chili pepper, minced

7 oz (200 g) baby octopus, finely chopped

1/2 cup (120 ml) white wine

parsley, minced

Mix the pasta dough ingredients together to form
a smooth dough. Wrap in plastic wrap and refrigerate
for 20 minutes.
Melt the butter for the filling and sauté the shallot.
Add the potatoes, salt and pepper and cook for
10 minutes, gradually adding the vegetable broth.
Once tender, add the thyme and puree the mixture
in a food processor.
Roll out the pasta dough into a thin sheet.
Place small piles of the potato mixture on half the sheet,
then fold over the other sheet and cut out ravioli using
a ravioli or cookie cutter. Make and X-shaped incision on
the bottom of the tomatoes and blanch in boiling water
for 2 minutes. Drain, immerse in ice water, drain again
and peel. Dice the flesh. Heat the olive oil for the sauce
and sauté the garlic and chile. Remove the garlic and add
the octopus. Sauté for 2 minutes, then add the tomatoes
and wine. Bring a large pot of salted water to a boil
and cook the ravioli. Drain and toss with the octopus
sauce. Serve hot, sprinkled with parsley.

Preparation time **30 minutes**
Cooking time **20 minutes**
Level **easy**
Wine **Etna Bianco**

pear and ricotta ravioli with pecorino

Ingredients for 4 servings

Pasta dough:

5 eggs

1 tbsp extra-virgin olive oil, salt

4½ cups (1 lb or 500 g) all-purpose flour

Filling:

1 lb (500 g) Ricotta

1 pear, peeled and diced, **2** egg yolks

1 cup (3½ oz or 100 g) grated Parmesan cheese

Sauce:

10½ oz (300 g) semi-aged pecorino cheese, shaved

1 pear, peeled and thinly sliced

1/2 cup plus 2½ tbsps (5½ oz or 150 g) butter, melted

poppy seeds

Beat eggs in a large bowl then add oil, salt and flour a little at a time. Mix to form a smooth and uniform dough. Let rest 30 minutes.
Mix together the Ricotta, pear, egg yolks and Parmesan.
Roll out the dough using a pasta machine.
Cut the dough into 4-inch (10 cm) rounds.
Place 1 tablespoon of the filling on each circle and fold in half. Press down around the edges to seal.
Bring a large pot of salted water to boil.
Boil the ravioli for a few minutes then drain carefully.
Transfer the ravioli to a serving dish.
Top with pecorino shavings, pear slices and the melted butter. Sprinkle with poppy seeds and serve immediately.

Preparation time **1 hour**
Cooking time **10 minutes**
Level **medium**
Wine **Bianco d'Alcamo**

perch ravioli with orange butter

Ingredients for 4 servings

Filling:

3½ tbsps (2 oz or 50 g) butter

1 garlic clove, minced

4 anchovies in oil, drained

10½ oz (300 g) perch fillets, chopped

1/2 cup (120 ml) white wine, **1** egg, salt

Pasta dough:

2 cups (9 oz or 250 g) all-purpose flour

2 eggs

Sauce:

2 organic oranges

3½ tbsps (2 oz or 50 g) butter

parsley, minced

Melt the butter for the filling and sauté the garlic.
Add the anchovies, then the perch. Cook over low heat,
seasoning with salt and adding the white wine.
Cover and cook for 10 minutes, adding a little water
if necessary. Mince the fish in a meat mincer or a food
processor, stir in the egg and set aside.
Mix together the flour and eggs to make a smooth dough.
Roll out the dough into a thin sheet.
Place small piles of the perch mixture on half the sheet,
then fold over the other sheet and cut out ravioli using
a ravioli or cookie cutter.
Cut julienne strips of orange zest, then squeeze
the oranges.
Bring a large pot of salted water to a boil and cook
the ravioli.Melt the butter in a frying pan and add the
orange juice. Drain the ravioli and toss with the butter
and orange juice. Sprinkle with parsley and the julienned
orange zest.

Perch are native to North America, and
are one of the most prized freshwater
fish. Generally they are sold already filleted because the dorsal fin bones and
the gills make it hard to fillet at home.

Preparation time **35 minutes**
Cooking time **20 minutes**
Level **medium**
Wine **Inzolia**

salmon ravioli with asparagus and cilantro

Ingredients for 4 servings

Pasta dough:

2⅓ cups plus 1 tbsp
(10½ oz or 300 g) all-purpose flour

3 eggs, **1** tbsp extra-virgin olive oil

Filling:

10½ oz (300 g) salmon fillet, diced

4½ oz (125 g) ricotta

1 dill sprig, minced

salt and pepper

Sauce:

10 asparagus spears

2 tbsps (1 oz or 30 g) butter

1/2 cup (120 ml) heavy cream

1 fresh cilantro sprig, minced

salt and freshly ground black pepper

Mix the pasta dough ingredients together to form a smooth dough. Wrap in plastic wrap and refrigerate for 20 minutes.
Mix together the salmon, ricotta and dill and season with salt and pepper.
Roll the pasta dough out thinly and cut into long strips. Place spoonfuls of the salmon mixture about 2 inches (5 cm) apart along half of the strips, then cover with the other strips.
Press down around the filling and cut out ravioli.
Slice the asparagus stalks, keeping the tips whole. Set aside the tips. Heat the butter and sauté the sliced stalks. Season with salt and pepper and cook until tender. Puree half the asparagus then return to the pan with the rest. Add the cream and cook until thickened. Season to taste with salt.
Bring a large pot of salted water to a boil and cook the ravioli together with the asparagus tips.
Drain and toss with the asparagus sauce.
Sprinkle with cilantro and freshly ground black pepper.

Preparation time **40 minutes**
Cooking time **20 minutes**
Level **easy**
Wine **Terre di Franciacorta Bianco**

langoustine ravioli in foie gras sauce

Ingredients for 4 servings

Sauce:

2 tbsps extra-virgin olive oil

3 shallots, unpeeled and halved

3/4 cup (180 ml) Port wine

1/2 cup (120 ml) Cognac

4 cups (1 litre) chicken demi-glace

10 black peppercorns, crushed, salt

4 cups (1 litre) heavy cream

9 oz (250 g) foie gras terrine, chopped

Filling:

1 tab of butter

2 tbsps extra-virgin olive oil

1 lb (500 g) very fresh langoustines, shelled

salt and pepper, **1** egg white, beaten

Pasta dough:

12½ oz (350 g) egg pasta dough

Garnish:

1 tbsp minced black truffle

Heat the olive oil for the sauce in a saucepan and sauté the halved shallots. Add the Port and Cognac and cook down until reduced to less than half the original volume. Add the chicken demi-glace, peppercorns and salt.
Add the cream and continue cooking until reduced to less than 4 cups (1 litre).
Strain the sauce, then place over a double boiler. Gradually whisk in the chopped foie gras terrine. Whisk until smooth, then remove from the heat and let cool. Heat the butter and olive oil for the filling and sauté the langoustines. Season with salt and pepper, then let cool. Roll out the pasta dough into a thin sheet and cut into circles. Place a langoustine in the center of each circle. Brush the edges with egg white and bring them together, pinching to seal.
Bring a large pot of salted water to a boil and cook the ravioli. Drain and transfer to heated plates. Reheat the sauce, pour over the ravioli, and sprinkle with a little minced truffle.

Preparation time **20 minutes**
Cooking time **25 minutes**
Level **medium**
Wine **Metodo Classico Franciacorta Dosaggio Zero**

rabbit and apple ravioli
with white truffle

Ingredients for 4 servings
Pasta dough:

1½ cups (8 oz or 220 g) all-purpose flour

6 egg yolks, **1** pinch of saffron

Sauce:

1 tab of butter, hot vegetable broth

1/2 small white onion, minced

1 large yellow-fleshed potato, peeled and thinly sliced

Filling:

3 tbsps extra-virgin olive oil

1 shallot, minced, **4** rabbit legs

1 tbsp white wine

1 Golden Delicious apple, peeled and diced

1 rosemary sprig, salt and pepper

Garnish:

1 white truffle, shaved

Mix the pasta dough ingredients together to form a smooth dough. Wrap in plastic wrap and refrigerate for 30 minutes.Melt the butter for the sauce and sauté the onion. Add the potato and cover with hot broth. Cook for 20 minutes, then puree until smooth.
Heat the olive oil for the filling and sauté the shallot. Add the rabbit and let brown, then add the wine, apple and rosemary. Cook for 15 minutes, seasoning with salt and pepper. Remove the rabbit from the pan and debone. Dice the meat. Drain the apples from the cooking liquid (reserving the liquid) and mix the rabbit and apples together in a bowl, seasoning to taste with salt and pepper.
Roll out the dough into a thin sheet. Place small piles of the rabbit-apple mixture on half the sheet, then fold the dough over and cut out ravioli using a ravioli or cookie cutter. Bring a large pot of salted water to a boil and cook the ravioli. Drain and toss in a frying pan with the reserved cooking liquid. Serve the ravioli over the potato sauce, topped with white truffle shavings.

Preparation time **50 minutes**
Cooking time **45 minutes**
Level **medium**
Wine **Alto Adige Santa Maddalena**

Filled Pasta

244

whole-wheat broccoli ravioli
with shrimp and olives

Ingredients for 4 servings

Filling:

1 large head of broccoli, cut into florets

4 tbsps extra-virgin olive oil

dried red chili pepper flakes

salt and pepper

Pasta dough:

2 cups (9 oz or 250 g) all-purpose flour

1 cup plus 3 tbsps (5½ oz or 150 g) whole-wheat flour

2 eggs plus 3 egg yolks

Sauce:

20 shrimp, **1** bay leaf

3 tbsps extra-virgin olive oil

1 garlic clove, **4** tomatoes, chopped

1 cup (3½ oz or 100 g) chopped broccoli

10 Taggiasca or other black olives, pitted

3½ tbsps (2 oz or 50 g) butter

salt and pepper

Boil the broccoli for the filling until tender, then drain and puree in a food processor with the oil, chile, salt and pepper.

Mix together all the pasta dough ingredients to make smooth dough. Divide the dough in half and roll out into 2 thin sheets. Place spoonfuls of the broccoli puree at regular intervals on the first sheet, and brush between them with water. Top with the second sheet and press down between the filling. Cut out ravioli.

Shell and devein the shrimp, reserving the shells. Boil the shells in water with the bay leaf to make a broth, then strain.

Chop the shrimp and sauté them in the olive oil with the garlic, tomatoes, chopped broccoli and olives. Add a little of the shrimp broth and adjust salt and pepper. Remove from the heat Bring a large pot of salted water to a boil and cook the ravioli. Drain and add to the sauce with the butter. Sauté until the sauce becomes creamy. Serve hot.

Preparation time **1 hour**
Cooking time **20 minutes**
Level **medium**
Wine **Trentino Nosiola**

spicy ravioli with clams

Ingredients for 4 servings
Pasta dough:
1¾ cups (8 oz or 220 g) all-purpose flour

2 eggs

1 tbsp extra-virgin olive oil

2 tbsps finely ground cornmeal

1/4 cup (2 oz or 50 g) boiled spinach

Filling and sauce:
3 potatoes, peeled

2 tbsps extra-virgin olive oil

2 garlic cloves, minced

1 red chili pepper, minced

1 lb (500 g) clams, parsley, minced

1/2 cup (120 ml) white wine

1 tbsp grated Parmesan cheese

1 egg, salt and pepper

Garnish:
cherry tomatoes, quartered

Mix together the flour, eggs and olive oil to make a dough. Divide in half. Mix the cornmeal into half the dough, and the spinach into the other half.
Form into balls, wrap in plastic wrap and refrigerate. Thinly slice 2 potatoes and dice the third.
Heat 1 tablespoon olive oil with the garlic, chile and parsley. Add the clams and wine and cover. Cook for 6-7 minutes. Cook the sliced potatoes in 1 ladleful of the clam cooking liquid until they are falling apart. Stir in the Parmesan and egg and season with salt and pepper. Roll out the different pasta doughs into thin sheets. Cover the yellow sheet with small spoonfuls of the potato mixture. Lay the green sheet on top and use a flower-shaped cookie cutter to cut out ravioli.
Heat 1 tablespoon olive oil and sauté the diced potato. Add to the clams. Remove some of the clam shells. Bring a large pot of salted water to a boil and cook the ravioli for 3 minutes. Drain and transfer to the pan with the clams and continue cooking until the sauce is slightly thickened. Garnish with cherry tomatoes and serve.

Preparation time **40 minutes**
Cooking time **15 minutes**
Level **medium**
Wine **Ribolla Gialla**

green ravioli with shrimp in fresh tomato sauce

Ingredients for 4 servings

Pasta dough:

1/2 cup (3½ oz or 100 g) boiled spinach

2 eggs, salt

2 cups (9 oz or 250 g) all-purpose flour

Filling:

2 slices of sandwich bread

3 tbsps heavy cream

1 lb (500 g) shrimp

1 tbsp minced parsley, salt and pepper

Sauce:

6 tbsps extra-virgin olive oil

2/3 cup (3 oz or 80 g) minced celery, carrot and shallot

1 parsley sprig, **1** tsp tomato paste

2 tbsps brandy

1½ cups (7 oz or 200 g) cherry tomatoes, halved

Puree the spinach with the eggs and a pinch of salt in a blender or food processor. Mix with the flour to form a smooth dough. Wrap in plastic wrap and refrigerate for 20 minutes. Soak the bread in the cream until soft, then drain. Shell the shrimp, reserving the shells. Puree the shrimp with the soaked bread and parsley and season with salt and pepper. Heat 2 tablespoons olive oil and sauté the celery, carrot and shallot.
Add the shrimp shells, parsley sprig and tomato paste. Pour over the brandy, cover with water and let simmer for 35 minutes. Strain the broth. Divide the dough in half and roll out into 2 thin sheets. Place spoonfuls of the shrimp puree at regular intervals on the first sheet, and brush between them with water. Lay over the second sheet and press down between the filling. Cut out ravioli.
Heat the remaining 4 tablespoons olive oil in a frying pan. Add the cherry tomatoes, sauté briefly, then add the shrimp broth. Cook for 15 minutes. Bring a large pot of salted water to a boil and cook the ravioli until al dente. Drain and add to the pan with the tomatoes. Sauté for 1 minute, then serve.

Preparation time **1 hour**
Cooking time **1 hour**
Level **easy**
Wine **Lugana**

potato, shrimp and caciotta ravioli

Ingredients for 4 servings

Sauce:

1½ cups (7 oz or 200 g)
cherry tomatoes

2 tbsps extra-virgin olive oil

1 garlic clove, peeled
fresh basil leaves, salt

Pasta dough:

1¼ cups plus 3 tbsps
(6½ oz or 180 g) all-purpose flour

5 egg yolks

Filling:

9 oz (250 g) new potatoes, salt

7 oz (200 g) shrimp, shelled and diced

2 oz (50 g) caciotta cheese,
diced, or ricotta

3 chervil or parsley leaves, minced

2 tbsps extra-virgin olive oil

Chervil is an aromatic herb with a
unique fragrance and can be used like
parsley, though it is rarely cooked.

Place the cherry tomatoes in a heavy-bottomed saucepan
with the olive oil, whole garlic clove, basil and salt.
Cover and cook for 35-40 minutes, without stirring.
Meanwhile mix the flour and egg yolks together to form
a smooth dough. Wrap in plastic wrap and refrigerate.
Boil the new potatoes in salted water and drain as soon
as they are tender. Dice them and mix with the shrimp,
cheese, chervil, olive oil and salt.
Roll the pasta out as thinly as possible and cut out many
circles with a cookie cutter. Place spoonfuls of the shrimp
mixture on half the circles, brush around the edges with
water and top with the other half. Press down well to seal.
Drain any excess oil from the tomatoes and pass them
through a food mill, or puree and strain.
Bring a large pot of salted water to a boil and cook
the ravioli until al dente.
Drain and serve over the tomato sauce.

Preparation time **45 minutes**
Cooking time **50 minutes**
Level **easy**
Wine **Bianchello del Metauro**

steamed broccoli ravioli with scallops

Ingredients for 4 servings

Pasta dough:

2⅓ cups plus 1 tbsp (10½ oz or 300 g) all-purpose flour

3 tbsps water, **2** tbsps milk

1 tbsp extra-virgin olive oil, salt

Filling:

10 cherry tomatoes

1 head of broccoli, cut into small florets

1 tbsp capers, chopped

10 black olives, pitted and chopped

Sauce:

1 tbsp extra-virgin olive oil

1 shallot, minced, **10** scallops, quartered

1/2 cup (120 ml) white wine

1 tbsp heavy cream

Garnish:

thyme leaves

Mix the pasta dough ingredients together to form a smooth dough. Wrap in plastic wrap and refrigerate for at least 20 minutes.

Blanch the cherry tomatoes for 2 minutes in boiling water, then peel, deseed and chop.

Steam the broccoli florets until tender.

Roll the pasta dough out thinly into 2 sheets. Make small mounds with 1 broccoli floret, a few pieces of tomato and a little chopped caper and olive on one of the sheets. Lay over the other sheet, press around the filling to remove any air, and cut into large ravioli.

Place in a steaming basket and steam for 8 minutes. Meanwhile heat the olive oil in a saucepan and sauté the shallot until golden. Add the scallops and white wine and continue cooking for 5 minutes.

Remove from the heat and stir in the cream.

Serve the ravioli with the scallop sauce, garnished with thyme leaves.

Preparation time **50 minutes**
Cooking time **35 minutes**
Level **medium**
Wine **Alto Adige Pinot Bianco**

walnut tortelli with artichokes

Ingredients for 4 servings

Pasta dough:

1½ cups plus 1½ tbsps
(7 oz or 200 g) all-purpose flour

1/2 cup (2 oz or 60 g) chestnut flour

3 eggs, salt, **1** tbsp extra-virgin olive oil

Filling:

1/4 cup (1 oz or 30 g) walnuts

7 oz (200 g) Ricotta

6 tbsps grated Pecorino cheese

1 egg yolk, salt and pepper

Sauce:

4 small artichokes

2 tbsps extra-virgin olive oil

1 garlic clove, salt

Garnish:

3½ tbsps (2 oz or 50 g) butter

2 tbsps grated Parmesan

chervil (optional)

Mix all the pasta dough ingredients together. Knead
to form a smooth dough. Cover and let rest for 30 minutes.
Toast the walnuts and chop finely.
Mix the ricotta with the Pecorino and egg yolk.
Add the walnuts and season with salt and pepper.
Roll out the pasta dough and make tortelli with the walnut
filling. Place the tortelli on a floured baking sheet.
Cut the stalks off the artichokes and trim them, removing
the hard external leaves and the choke.
Quarter and thinly slice.
Sauté the artichokes with the olive oil and whole garlic
clove. Season with salt, cover and cook for 10 minutes.
Bring a large pot of salted water to a boil and cook
the tortelli for 3-4 minutes.
Meanwhile, brown the butter in a frying pan.
Drain the tortelli and transfer them to a serving bowl.
Add the brown butter and top with artichokes and grated
Parmesan. Garnish with chervil if desired.

Preparation time **40 minutes**
Cooking time **15 minutes**
Level **medium**
Wine **Dolcetto di Dogliani**

duck foie gras and apple tortelli

Ingredients for 4 servings
Pasta dough:
4 cups (1 lb plus 1½ oz or 500 g)
all-purpose flour
7 eggs, **1** tbsp extra-virgin olive oil, salt

Filling:
3½ tbsps (2 oz or 50 g) butter
2 apples, peeled and diced
7 oz (200 g) duck foie gras, diced
1/4 cup (60 ml) Cognac, salt and pepper

Sauce:
3½ tbsps (2 oz or 50 g) butter
2/3 cup (3½ oz or 100 g)
thinly sliced shallot
2/3 cup (3½ oz or 100 g)
thinly sliced onion
2 cups (500 ml) beef broth
1 cup (3½ oz or 100 g) grated
Parmesan cheese

Garnish:
chervil leaves

Mound the flour on a work surface and make a well
in the middle. Break in the eggs, add the olive oil and salt,
and mix together to form a smooth dough. Roll the dough
into a thin sheet and cut out equal-sized squares.
Melt the butter for the filling in a saucepan and sauté
the apples. Deglaze with 1 tablespoon Cognac.
Place a small amount of foie gras and apples in the center
of half the dough squares. Season with salt and pepper.
Brush the edges with the remaining Cognac before closing
up with the remaining dough squares. Press down to seal.
Melt the butter in a saucepan and sauté the shallot
and onion over low heat for 10 minutes.
Add the broth and cook for another 10 minutes.
Bring a large pot of salted water to a boil and cook
the tortelli. Drain, toss with Parmesan and serve
with the soupy shallot and onion sauce.
Garnish with chervil.

Preparation time **30 minutes**
Cooking time **25 minutes**
Level **medium**
Wine **Vermentino della Riviera Ligure di Ponente Pigato**

pumpkin tortelli
with butter and sage

Ingredients for 4 servings

Pasta dough:

1½ cups plus **1½** tbsps
(7 oz or 200 g) all-purpose flour

1 egg plus 2 egg yolks

1 tbsp extra-virgin olive oil, salt

Filling:

2 tbsps (1 oz or 30 g) butter

2 amaretti cookies, **1/2** onion, minced

2 cups (9 oz or 250 g) diced pumpkin
or other winter squash

3/4 cup (180 ml) hot vegetable broth

2 tbsps grated Parmesan cheese

nutmeg, salt and pepper

Sauce:

2 slices smoked pancetta
or bacon, julienned

3½ tbsps (2 oz or 50 g) butter

sage leaves

Mix all the pasta dough ingredients together. Knead to form a smooth dough. Cover and let rest for 20 minutes. Melt the butter for the filling and sauté the onion.
Add the pumpkin and cook over low heat, gradually adding hot broth. As soon as the pumpkin is tender, puree in a food processor with the amaretti. Stir in the Parmesan, freshly grated nutmeg, salt and pepper.
Roll the pasta dough out thinly into 2 sheets.
Place spoonfuls of the filling on one of the sheets, about 1 inch (2½ cm) apart from each other.
Cover with the second sheet and press around the filling with fingertips. Cut out with a rolling cutter and set aside.
Sauté the pancetta with the butter and sage.
Bring a large pot of salted water to a boil and cook the tortelli. Drain and toss in the pan with the pancetta, adding a little of the cooking water. Serve immediately.

Preparation time **40 minutes**
Cooking time **30 minutes**
Level **easy**
Wine **Val Venosta Riesling**

potato ravioli with sea bream ragù

Ingredients for 4 servings

Pasta dough:

2⅓ cups plus 1 tbsp
(10½ oz or 300 g) all-purpose flour

2 eggs plus 2 egg yolks

Filling:

1 potato (about 7 oz or 200 g)

1 tab of butter, 1 shallot, minced

6 black olives, pitted and finely chopped

1 thyme sprig, leaves only

1 tbsp grated Parmesan cheese, salt

Sauce:

2 tbsps extra-virgin olive oil

1 garlic clove

9 oz (250 g) sea bream fillet, skinned,
deboned and chopped

6 cherry tomatoes, quartered

parsley, minced, salt and pepper

Garnish:

basil, julienned (optional)

Mix the flour, eggs and egg yolks together. Knead to form a smooth dough. Cover and let rest for 30 minutes.
Boil the potato, peel and mash.
Melt the butter and sauté the shallot, together with a little water, until transparent.
Mix together the sautéed shallot, mashed potato, olives, thyme, Parmesan and a little salt and stir well.
Roll the pasta dough out thinly into 2 sheets.
Place spoonfuls of the filling on one of the sheets, about 1 inch (2½ cm) apart from each other.
Cover with the second sheet and press around the filling with fingertips. Cut out with a serrated cutter and set aside in a cool place.
Heat the olive oil for the sauce in a frying pan and sauté the garlic. Add the sea bream, then the tomatoes and a little parsley. Season with salt and pepper and add a little water. Continue cooking until the fish is cooked through. Bring a large pot of salted water to a boil and cook the ravioli. Drain and toss in the frying pan with the sauce. Garnish with julienned basil, if desired, and serve.

Preparation time **30 minutes**
Cooking time **40 minutes**
Level **easy**
Wine **Bolgheri Bianco**

Filled Pasta

guinea hen tortelli
with raisins and marsala

Ingredients for 4 servings

Pasta dough:

1¾ cups (8 oz or 220 g)
all-purpose flour

2 eggs, 2 tbsps boiled spinach, pureed

1 tbsp extra-virgin olive oil, salt

Filling:

2 tbsps (1 oz or 30 g) butter

1/2 leek, minced, 1 carrot, minced

1 celery stalk, minced

1/2 guinea 1/2, deboned and chopped

thyme leaves, pepper

2 tbsps Marsala wine

2 tbsps heavy cream

Sauce:

1 pat of butter, 2 tbsps raisins

2 tbsps Marsala wine, salt and pepper

3 tbsps grated Parmesan cheese

Mound the flour on a work surface and make a well in the middle. Break in the eggs, add the spinach, salt and olive oil, and mix together to form a smooth dough.
Wrap in plastic wrap and refrigerate for 20 minutes.
Melt the butter for the filling and sauté the leek, carrot and celery. Add the guinea hen, thyme and pepper and sauté for 20 minutes. Add the Marsala and let evaporate. Remove from the heat and let cool, then puree in a food processor with the cream.
Roll the pasta dough out thinly into 2 sheets.
Place spoonfuls of the filling on one of the sheets, about 1 inch (2½ cm) apart from each other. Cover with the second sheet and press around the filling with fingertips. Cut out with a scalloped cutter and close each tortello around a finger. Bring a large pot of salted water to a boil and cook the tortelli. Meanwhile melt the butter for the sauce and add the raisins. Add the Marsala and a little salt and pepper, and a little of the pasta cooking water.
Drain the ravioli and add to the pan.
Sauté together with the Parmesan.

Preparation time **35 minutes**
Cooking time **45 minutes**
Level **medium**
Wine **Nebbiolo d'Alba**

tortellini with herbed ricotta and crispy artichokes

Ingredients for 4 servings

Pasta dough:

1½ cups plus 1½ tbsps
(7 oz or 200 g) all-purpose flour

2 tbsps extra-virgin olive oil

2 eggs, salt

Filling:

4 oz (110 g) prosciutto, chopped

1 tbsp grated Parmesan cheese

2 tbsps minced parsley

1 tbsp breadcrumbs, 1 egg yolk

2 tbsps extra-virgin olive oil, salt

Ricotta:

7 oz (200 g) sheep's milk ricotta

thyme, minced, chives, minced

salt and pepper, nutmeg

Artichokes:

2 baby artichokes, sunflower oil

Broth:

beef broth

Mix all the pasta dough ingredients together. Knead to form a smooth dough. Cover and let rest for 30 minutes. Mince together the prosciutto, Parmesan, parsley, breadcrumbs and egg yolk in a food processor.
Add the olive oil and adjust the salt. Roll the dough out using a pasta machine.
Place spoonfuls of the prosciutto mixture on half the sheet of dough, then fold over the other half and press around the filling. Cut out into triangles and wrap around the finger to form tortellini. Pass the ricotta through a sieve and beat it with thyme, chives, salt and pepper. Add freshly grated nutmeg to taste. Form the ricotta into circles in the center of each plate, using a cookie cutter. Trim the artichokes and thinly slice them.
Heat the sunflower oil until very hot then fry the artichoke slices until golden-brown. Drain on paper towels.
Bring the beef broth to a boil and cook the tortellini. Drain, reserving the broth, and place the tortellini around the ricotta. Top with crispy artichokes and finish with 2 spoonfuls of the hot broth.

Preparation time **30 minutes**
Cooking time **15 minutes**
Level **medium**
Wine **Bianco Capena**

artichoke tortelloni
with melted onions

Ingredients for 4 servings
Pasta dough:

1½ cups plus **1½** tbsps
(7 oz or 200 g) all-purpose flour

3/4 cup (3½ oz or 100 g)
whole-wheat flour

3 eggs, salt

Filling:

2 tbsps extra-virgin olive oil

1 garlic clove, **7** oz (200 g) ricotta

4 artichoke hearts, cut into wedges

2 tbsps grated Parmesan cheese

salt and pepper

Sauce:

2 tbsps (1 oz or 30 g) butter

2 white onions, thinly sliced

salt and pepper

2 tbsps grated Parmesan cheese

2 tbsps extra-virgin olive oil

1 marjoram sprig, leaves only

Mix all the pasta dough ingredients together. Knead
to form a smooth dough. Cover and let rest for 30 minutes.
Heat the olive oil for the filling and sauté the garlic.
Add the artichokes and sauté, adding a little water, until
tender. Remove from the heat, let cool and finely chop.
Stir the ricotta, artichokes and Parmesan together
and season with salt and pepper.
Roll out the dough into a thin sheet.
Cut out circles with a diameter of about 3 inches (6-8 cm).
Top them with the artichoke-ricotta mixture and fold
in half to form tortelloni.
Melt the butter for the sauce and add the onions. Let cook
very gently, without letting them color. Season with salt,
add 4 tablespoons water and continue cooking until they
are transparent and very soft. Puree the onions with the
Parmesan and olive oil until smooth.
Bring a large pot of lightly salted water to a boil and cook
the tortelloni. Drain and toss with the onion puree.
Sprinkle with pepper and marjoram leaves.
Sauté for 1 minute.

Preparation time **40 minutes**
Cooking time **30 minutes**
Level **medium**
Wine **Alto Adige Pinot Grigio**

Filled Pasta

spinach ravioli in carrot sauce

Ingredients for 4 servings

Pasta dough:

1½ cups plus 1½ tbsps
(7 oz or 200 g) all-purpose flour

2 eggs, salt

Filling:

1 egg yolk, **1** lb (500 g) spinach

10½ oz (300 g) sheep's milk ricotta

2 tbsps grated Parmesan cheese

nutmeg, salt and pepper

Sauce:

1 tbsp extra-virgin olive oil

1 shallot, minced

4 carrots, peeled and sliced

1/2 cup (180 ml) vegetable broth

salt and pepper

3½ tbsps (2 oz or 50 g) butter

1½ oz (40 g) aged Parmesan
cheese, shaved

Mix together the flour and eggs with a little salt to obtain a smooth dough. Wrap in plastic wrap and refrigerate for 30 minutes.
Boil the spinach until tender.
Drain, squeeze out excess liquid, and chop finely. Mix with the ricotta, egg yolk and grated Parmesan. Season with freshly grated nutmeg, salt and pepper to taste.
Roll out the pasta dough with a rolling pin or a pasta machine. Place spoonfuls of the spinach mixture on one of the sheets, about 1 inch (2½ cm) apart from each other. Cover with the second sheet and press around the filling with fingertips. Cut out with a fluted cutter.
Heat the olive oil for the sauce and sauté the shallot. Add the carrots and cover with broth. Season with salt and pepper and let cook until almost falling apart, about 15 minutes, then puree in a food processor. Keep warm. Melt the butter in a saucepan.
Bring a large pot of salted water to a boil and cook the tortelli. Drain and toss with the melted butter, then serve with the hot carrot sauce and Parmesan shavings.

Preparation time **30 minutes**
Cooking time **30 minutes**
Level **medium**
Wine **Trentino Nosiola**

pumpkin cappellacci with beef ragù

Ingredients for 6 servings

Sauce:

2 tbsps (1 oz or 30 g) butter
1 onion, minced, **1** carrot, minced
1 celery stalk, minced
3½ oz (100 g) pancetta or bacon, diced
10½ oz (300 g) ground beef
3/4 cup (180 ml) red wine
salt and pepper
6 tbsps ready-made tomato sauce
grated Parmesan cheese (optional)

Pasta dough:

4 cups (1 lb plus 1½ oz or 500 g)
all-purpose flour
5 eggs, salt

Filling:

3⅓ lb (1½ kg) pumpkin or yellow
winter squash, peeled, deseeded
and chopped
2 cups (7 oz or 200 g) grated
Parmesan cheese
nutmeg, salt

Melt the butter in a large frying pan and sauté the onion, carrot and celery. Add the pancetta and sauté for a few minutes, then add the beef and let brown well. Add the red wine, salt and pepper. Once the red wine has cooked off, add the tomato sauce. Cook for 3 hours.
Preheat the oven to 400°F (200°C or Gas Mark 6).
Mix all the pasta dough ingredients together. Knead to form a smooth dough. Cover and let rest for 30 minutes. Arrange the pumpkin on a baking tray and roast for a few minutes, until soft. Remove from the oven, transfer to a bowl and mash with a fork to form a puree.
Stir in the Parmesan, a pinch of freshly grated nutmeg and a pinch of salt. Roll the dough out into a thin sheet, cut into squares and place a tablespoon of pumpkin filling in the center of each one. Form the cappellacci by folding the squares into triangles, press down along the edges to seal and bringing two opposite corners together, pressing down to adhere. Bring a large pot of salted water to a boil and cook the cappellacci. Drain and serve with the ragù, sprinkled with Parmesan if desired.

Preparation time **45 minutes**
Cooking time **3 hours 5 minutes**
Level **medium**
Wine **Colli Bolognesi Merlot**

chard and ricotta tortelli

Ingredients for 6 servings

Filling and sauce:

1½ lb (700 g) Swiss chard

10½ oz (300 g) ricotta

1/3 cup (3 oz or 80 g) melted butter

1 egg

2 cups (7 oz or 200 g) grated
Parmesan cheese

nutmeg, salt

Pasta dough:

4 cups (1 lb plus 1½ oz or 500 g)
all-purpose flour

4 eggs, salt

Trim the Swiss chard, removing the white stalk. Bring a pot of water to a boil and cook the chard for about 15 minutes, then drain and squeeze out excess liquid. Finely chop the chard. Mix together the ricotta, chard, 2 tbsps (1 oz or 30 g) melted butter, 1 egg and a handful of grated Parmesan. The mixture should be compact and smooth. Season with freshly grated nutmeg and salt. Mound the flour on a work surface and make a well in the middle. Break in the eggs and add a pinch of salt. Mix into a firm dough, adding as much water as necessary. Knead until smooth. Roll the dough out into a thin sheet and cut into strips 4 inches (10 cm) wide. Place little spoonfuls of the filling along one edge of the strips, about 2 inches (5 cm) apart, then fold over the strip to cover the filling. Press around the filling with the fingers to expel any air, and press firmly around the edges to stop any filling leaking out during cooking. Cut the tortelli into rectangles with a rolling cutter or cookie cutter. Bring a large pot of salted water to a boil. Cook the tortelli for 10 minutes, then drain. Make layers in a serving dish of tortelli, melted butter and grated Parmesan. Serve hot.

Preparation time **45 minutes**
Cooking time **25 minutes**
Level **easy**
Wine **Colli di Parma Sauvignon**

This is a typical first course from the area around Parma. It is traditionally made for the feast of San Giovanni on June 23, and always eaten al fresco.

Filled Pasta

274

potato tortelli with ragù

Ingredients for 4 servings

Pasta dough:

4 cups (1 lb plus 1½ oz or 500 g)
all-purpose flour

4 eggs

Filling:

2 lb (1 kg) potatoes, salt

2 tbsps extra-virgin olive oil

1 garlic clove, minced

1 egg , nutmeg, parsley, minced

2 tbsps ready-made tomato sauce

grated Parmesan cheese

Sauce:

beef ragù (see p. 272)

Mound the flour on a work surface and make a well in the center. Break in the eggs and add enough water to mix a smooth dough. Wrap in plastic wrap and refrigerate.
Boil the potatoes in salted water until tender.
Drain, peel and pass through a food mill or potato ricer to make a smooth mash.
Heat the olive oil with the garlic, a handful of parsley and a pinch of salt. Sauté for 5 minutes then add the tomato sauce and cook for a few more minutes.
Mix together the mashed potatoes, tomato mixture, egg, freshly grated nutmeg and Parmesan and season with salt. Stir well until thoroughly combined.
Roll the pasta dough out thinly into 2 sheets.
Place spoonfuls of the filling on one of the sheets.
Cover with the second sheet and press around the filling with fingertips. Cut out tortelli.
Bring a large pot of salted water to a boil and cook the tortelli. Reheat the ragù.
Drain the tortelli and serve with the hot ragù.

Alternatively, serve the tortelli with a simple melted butter and grated Parmesan sauce, or a light mushroom-based sauce.

Preparation time **20 minutes**
Cooking time **25 minutes**
Level **medium**
Wine **Alto Adige Santa Maddalena**

baked pasta

Pasta

cannelloni with fennel, ham and emmental

Ingredients for 4 servings

Pasta dough:

2⅓ cups plus 1 tbsp
(10½ oz or 300 g) all-purpose flour

3 eggs, salt

Filling:

2 fennel bulbs, cut into wedges

salt and pepper

1 tbsp extra-virgin olive oil

1 thyme sprig, leaves only

5½ oz (150 g) ham, thinly sliced

7 oz (200 g) Emmental cheese,
cut into strips

3 tbsps (1½ oz or 40 g) butter

Emmental is a Swiss cheese with a history dating back to the 15th century. It is one of the most copied cheese styles in the world, and the Swiss have chosen to protect their cheese by calling it Emmentaler and registering it as a protected name.

Mix together the flour, eggs and salt to form a smooth dough. Wrap in plastic wrap and refrigerate for 30 minutes.
Preheat the oven to 350°F (180°C or Gas Mark 4).
Boil the fennel wedges in salted water for 15 minutes, or steam them, until tender but still al dente.
Drain and roughly chop the fennel.
Heat the olive oil in a frying pan and sauté the fennel over high heat. Add the thyme leaves, salt and pepper and let cool. Roll the pasta dough out thinly and cut it into large rectangles. Bring a large pot of salted water to a boil and cook the pasta rectangles, then drain and dry on a kitchen towel. Top each pasta sheet with the fennel, ham and Emmental (reserving about a third of the cheese for the topping) and roll them up. Arrange in a buttered baking dish and top with the remaining cheese.
Bake for 20 minutes. Serve hot.

Preparation time **30 minutes**
Cooking time **45 minutes**
Level **easy**
Wine **Ribolla Gialla**

individual fennel and artichoke lasagnas with gorgonzola

Ingredients for 4 servings

Pasta dough:

1½ cups plus 1½ tbsps (7 oz or 200 g) all-purpose flour

2 eggs, salt

Sauce:

6 baby artichokes, juice of 1/2 lemon

2 fennel bulbs, chopped, salt and pepper

5½ oz (160 g) Gorgonzola cheese, chopped

2 tbsps extra-virgin olive oil, **1** garlic clove

2/3 cup (2 oz or 60 g) walnuts, chopped

3 tbsps (1½ oz or 40 g) butter

Gorgonzola is a blue cheese with a protected denomination of origin. It is made from cow's milk in northern Italy, and comes in two main varieties, dolce, mild, and piccante, sharp.

Preheat the oven to 375°F (190°C or Gas Mark 5). Mix together the flour, eggs and salt to form a smooth dough. Wrap in plastic wrap and refrigerate. Trim the artichokes, removing the hard outer leaves and inner choke, and soak in water and lemon juice. Boil the fennel in salted water for 15 minutes, until tender but still al dente. Drain, season with salt and pepper and place in a bowl. Stir in half the Gorgonzola. Drain the artichokes and slice thinly. Heat the olive oil and garlic and sauté the artichokes. Season with salt and pepper and cook for 5-6 minutes, adding a little water. Remove from the heat and turn onto a cutting board. Roughly chop them, then place in a bowl and stir in the walnuts. Roll out the pasta dough and cut into circles using a cookie cutter. Bring a large pot of salted water to a boil and cook the pasta circles for 2 minutes. Compose the individual lasaganas on a baking tray using the same cookie cutter as a mold, making alternating layers of pasta circles, the fennel mixture and the artichoke mixture. Top each one with some of the remaining Gorgonzola and bake for 5 minutes. Serve immediately.

Preparation time **40 minutes**
Cooking time **30 minutes**
Level **medium**
Wine **Malvasia Istriana**

lasagna with carrots and peas

Ingredients for 4 servings

Pasta dough:

3 tbsps extra-virgin olive oil

1 white onion, minced

5 large carrots, peeled and sliced

salt and pepper

4 cups (1 litre) vegetable broth

2 cups (10½ oz or 300 g) spring peas

nutmeg

14 oz (400 g) thick béchamel

5 tbsps grated Parmesan cheese

1 lb (500 g) fresh lasagna sheets

3 tbsps (1½ oz or 40 g) butter, chopped

The carrots could be replaced with 2 cups (7 oz or 200 g) diced pumpkin.

Preheat the oven to 375°F (190°C or Gas Mark 5).
Divide the olive oil and the onion between two medium saucepans. Sauté the onion in the two pans, adding a little broth if necessary to keep it from burning.
Add the carrots to one of the saucepans. Let brown then season with salt and pepper and cover with 2 cups (500 ml) broth. Let cook for 10 minutes. Add the peas to the other saucepan and brown for 2 minutes, then cover with broth. Season with salt and pepper and cook for 20 minutes. Puree the carrots and the peas separately in a food processor or with an immersion blender. Stir half the béchamel into each puree and adjust salt and pepper. Add a grating of nutmeg and 2 tablespoons Parmesan to each one and set aside. Bring a large pot of salted water to a boil. Add a little olive oil and cook the pasta sheets. Drain and dry on a kitchen towel. Compose the lasagna in a buttered baking dish, alternating the pasta with the two vegetable purees to create color contrasts. Sprinkle the top with the remaining Parmesan and tabs of butter. Bake for 30 minutes, then serve immediately.

Preparation time **30 minutes**
Cooking time **1 hour 10 minutes**
Level **easy**
Wine **Alto Adige Pinot Bianco**

gratinéed rigatoni with carrots, cheese and pancetta

Ingredients for 4 servings

Pasta dough:

3 tbsps extra-virgin olive oil

1 shallot, minced, salt and pepper

4 large carrots, peeled and thinly sliced

2 cups (500 ml) hot vegetable broth

2 oz (60 g) pancetta or bacon, diced

14 oz (400 g) rigatoni

2 tbsps grated Parmesan cheese

5½ oz (150 g) mild smoked Provola or other mild smoked cheese, diced

5½ oz (150 g) cow's milk mozzarella, diced

10 basil leaves

⌐ Immersion blenders are useful for pureeing various ingredients, particularly soups, as they can be used directly in the food container, whether a bowl or a pan.

Preheat the oven to 375°F (190°C or Gas Mark 5).
Heat 2 tablespoons olive oil in a saucepan and sauté the shallot over low heat until soft.
Add the carrots, season with salt and pepper and cover with hot broth.
Cook for 20 minutes, until almost falling apart, then puree in a food processor or with an immersion blender.
Heat 1 tablespoon olive oil in a non-stick frying pan and sauté the pancetta or bacon until browned.
Bring a large pot of salted water to a boil and cook the rigatoni until al dente.
Drain and toss in the frying pan with the pancetta or bacon, then transfer to a bowl.
Stir in the carrot puree, Parmesan and Provola, then transfer to a baking dish.
Top with the mozzarella and bake for about 15 minutes.

Preparation time **15 minutes**
Cooking time **35 minutes**
Level **easy**
Wine **Alto Adige Santa Maddalena**

mini penne timbales with peas, fennel and carrots

Ingredients for 4 servings

Pasta dough:

salt and pepper

2 carrots, peeled and diced

1 cup (5½ oz or 150 g) spring peas

7 oz (200 g) smooth pennette

1 tab of butter

1/2 small white onion, minced

1/2 fennel bulb, chopped

2 tbsps extra-virgin olive oil

4 oz (120 g) sheep's milk ricotta

1 egg

1 tbsp grated Parmesan cheese

Preheat the oven to 375°F (190°C or Gas Mark 5).
Bring a large pot of salted water to a boil and blanch
the carrots for 3 minutes. Drain with a slotted spoon.
Cook the peas in the same water for 6 minutes, then drain
with a slotted spoon.
Use the same water to cook the pennette, and drain when
al dente. Immerse in cold water to cool them.
Butter 4 individual aluminum molds and line the sides
with the pennette.
Heat the olive oil and sauté the onion until soft.
Add the fennel and cook until very soft and almost falling
apart, adding water as necessary. Season with salt
and pepper then puree in a food processor.
Stir the ricotta, egg, Parmesan, peas and carrots into
the fennel puree and adjust salt and pepper. Fill the molds
with the mixture, pressing it down with the back
of a spoon. Bake for about 12 minutes.
Unmold and serve immediately.

Baked Pasta

288

Did you know that sheep's milk ricotta
has less fat than regular cow's milk
ricotta? It can be made sweet or
salted or aged into a firm cheese.

Preparation time **20 minutes**
Cooking time **20 minutes**
Level **medium**
Wine **Alto Adige Pinot Bianco**

fennel and ditaloni gratin

Ingredients for 4 servings

Pasta dough:

2 small fennel bulbs, quartered

salt and pepper

12½ oz (350 g) ridged ditaloni
or other short pasta

1¼ cups (300 ml) milk

nutmeg

3 tbsps (1½ oz or 40 g) butter

1 tbsp all-purpose flour

2 tbsps grated Parmesan cheese

2 tbsps breadcrumbs

Preheat the oven to 400°F (200°C or Gas Mark 6).
Boil the fennel in salted water or steam it until tender
but still al dente. Drain and chop.
Meanwhile bring a large pot of salted water to a boil
and cook the pasta until al dente. Drain.
Heat the milk with some freshly grated nutmeg.
In another saucepan, melt the butter and stir in the flour.
Whisk in the hot milk and simmer until thickened.
Season with salt and pepper to taste.
Stir the pasta and sauce together and add the fennel
and Parmesan.
Transfer to a baking dish and top with breadcrumbs.
Bake for 20 minutes then serve.

This dish can be made richer by
stirring a good melting cheese
into the fennel and pasta mixture,
perhaps mozzarella or stracchino.

Preparation time **30 minutes**
Cooking time **40 minutes**
Level **medium**
Wine **Cirò Rosato**

gratinéed seafood crêpes

Ingredients for 4 servings

Crêpes:

1 egg, **1** cup (250 ml) milk

3/4 cup (3½ oz or 100 g)
all-purpose flour

butter

Filling:

1 lb (500 g) mixed shellfish
(clams, mussels, cockles)

1 medium squid, cleaned
and chopped

3 tbsps extra-virgin olive oil

1 garlic clove, minced

1/2 red chili pepper, minced

salt and pepper

Sauce:

1 cup (6½ oz or 180 g) canned
crushed tomatoes

fresh basil, salt and pepper

Beat the egg and the milk together and gradually whisk
in the flour. Let the batter rest for 30 minutes.
Preheat the oven to 400°F (200°C or Gas Mark 6).
Meanwhile wash the shellfish well, scrubbing them under
cold running water and debearding the mussels.
Heat the olive oil, garlic and chile in a large frying pan
and then add the shellfish and the squid. Cover and let
cook until the shells open. Remove the shells and chop
the meat with a knife. Season to taste with salt and pepper
Heat a small amount of butter in a non-stick frying pan.
Wipe it out with a paper towel, then pour in some
of the batter. Roll the pan around to coat evenly and cook
for 2 minutes. Using a spatula, gently free the edges
of the crêpe from the pan and flip it over. Cook for another
minute then lay on a clean kitchen towel to cool.
Continue making crêpes until the batter is finished.
Fill the crêpes with the seafood mixture and roll up.
Arrange in a baking dish. Cook the tomatoes with the basil
until reduced and thickened, then season with salt
and pepper. Pour over the crêpes and bake for 10 minutes.

Preparation time **30 minutes**
Cooking time **15 minutes**
Level **medium**
Wine **Soave Superiore**

herbed cannelloni with potatoes, goat's cheese and bresaola

Ingredients for 4 servings

Pasta dough:

2 cups (9 oz or 250 g) all-purpose flour

2 eggs, **1** tbsp extra-virgin olive oil

2 tbsps finely minced mixed herbs

Filling:

3 medium potatoes (about 1⅓ lb or 600 g), peeled

8½ oz (240 g) fresh goat's milk cheese

3 tbsps extra-virgin olive oil

salt and pepper

9 oz (250 g) bresaola, thinly sliced

Garnish:

4 vine-ripened tomatoes

4 tbsps extra-virgin olive oil

2 garlic cloves

salt and pepper

chives, minced

Mix together the pasta dough ingredients to make a smooth dough. Wrap in plastic wrap and refrigerate for 30 minutes. Preheat the oven to 350°F (180°C or Gas Mark 4). Boil the potatoes until tender. Drain and pass them through a potato ricer or mash with a potato masher. Stir in the goat's cheese and olive oil and adjust the salt and pepper. Roll the pasta dough out into thin sheets and cut them into rectangles. Bring a large pot of salted water to a boil and cook the pasta sheets. Drain, let cool and pat dry. Spread each rectangle with a thin layer of the potato mixture. Top with bresaola slices and then another layer of the potato mixture. Roll up the cannelloni, cut them into 4-inch (10 cm) lengths and arrange them in an oiled baking dish. Cover with aluminum foil and bake for 10-15 minutes. Meanwhile blanch the tomatoes in boiling water for 30 seconds. Drain, peel, deseed and dice. Heat the olive oil for the garnish with the garlic and add the tomatoes. Season with salt and pepper and cook for 5-6 minutes. Serve the cannelloni garnished with the tomato sauce and minced chives.

Preparation time **1 hour**
Cooking time **30 minutes**
Level **medium**
Wine **Pinot Grigio del Piave**

stuffed ziti

Ingredients for 4 servings
Ziti:

1 red bell pepper

1 bunch of Swiss chard

1 large knob of butter

1 garlic clove, unpeeled

3 oz (80 g) ricotta, **2** eggs

3 tbsps grated Pecorino di fossa cheese (see note)

salt

10½ oz (300 g) hard-wheat ziti

Roast the bell pepper under the broiler, then close in a plastic bag for 10 minutes. Peel, deseed and finely chop. Trim the Swiss chard leaves, wash them and slice thinly. Do not dry the leaves.
Heat the butter with the garlic and add the Swiss chard. Cover the pan and cook over low heat until tender. Discard the garlic and puree the chard in a food processor. Place the chard in one bowl and the peppers in another bowl. Add half the ricotta and 1 egg to each bowl and stir well. Add 1 tablespoon Pecorino di fossa cheese to the chard mixture. Cover the bowls and refrigerate.
Bring a large pot of salted water to a boil and cook the ziti until just al dente. Drain and cool.
Using a pastry syringe fill half the ziti with the chard mixture and half with the peppers. Arrange them criss-crossed on a baking tray lined with parchment paper. Sprinkle with the remaining Pecorino.
Gratiné under a pre-heated broiler for 5 minutes, then serve.

Pecorino di fossa is a sheep's milk cheese which is aged for a few months before being placed in natural-fiber sacks, layered leaves and hay, and buried in deep tuff pits to ferment for several months. It has a strong, distinctive taste, and can be replaced in this recipe with a very aged Parmesan.

Preparation time **30 minutes**
Cooking time **15 minutes**
Level **medium**
Wine **Colli Romani Bianco**

saffron conchiglioni gratinéed with truffled reblochon

Ingredients for 4 servings

Conchiglioni:

6 cups (1½ l) vegetable broth

1 pinch of saffron

8½ oz (240 g) conchiglioni (giant pasta shells)

7 oz (200 g) Reblochon or other melting cheese

6 tbsps truffle oil

1 tab of butter

1 black truffle, shaved

Bring the broth to a boil and dissolve the saffron in it. Cook the conchiglioni in the broth and drain them when al dente. Reserve the cooking liquid.
Cool the pasta under cold water and set aside.
Pre-heat the broiler.
Slice the cheese into 1/5-inch (1/2 cm) slices and brush them with truffle oil.
Butter a baking dish and arrange the conchiglioni on the bottom.
Top with a few spoonfuls of the cooking liquid.
Lay the cheese slices on top and sprinkle with shaved truffle. Broil for 10 minutes, until the cheese forms a golden crust. Remove from the oven and serve hot.

Saffron was once called gold dust, and has been used in cooking for centuries. Already in 1450 it was a common ingredient for Martino de Rossi, author of one of one of the first Italian cookbooks and chef to the Sforza family.

Preparation time **15 minutes**
Cooking time **15 minutes**
Level **easy**
Wine **Trentino Marzemino**

spinach parcels with robiola

Ingredients for 4 servings
Pasta dough:
2 cups (2 oz or 50 g) spinach, salt
1½ cups plus 1½ tbsps (7 oz or 200 g) all-purpose flour
2 eggs
1 tbsp extra-virgin olive oil
Filling:
9 oz (250 g) Robiola di Roccaverano cheese (see note)
6 tbsps grated Parmesan cheese
1 tbsp extra-virgin olive oil
nutmeg, salt and pepper
Garnish:
fried artichokes (optional)

The origins of Robiola di Roccaverano cheese are lost in the mists of time. Produced near Asti, in the northwestern region of Piedmont, it is made from a mix of cow's, goat's and sheep's milk, and is soft and creamy. In this recipe it can be replaced with a fresh goat's milk cheese.

Preheat the oven to 325°F (170°C or Gas Mark 3).
Blanch the spinach in boiling salted water, drain and squeeze out excess liquid. Finely chop the spinach.
Mound the flour on a work surface and make a well in the center. Add the eggs, spinach and olive oil and mix together to form an elastic dough.
Wrap in plastic wrap and refrigerate.
Beat the Robiola with 4 tablespoons grated Parmesan, the olive oil, freshly grated nutmeg, salt and pepper until creamy.
Roll the pasta dough out with a rolling pin until very thin. Spread with the cheese mixture, then roll up into a long roll. Cut into lengths with a knife, in such a way that the pressure of the knife seals down the two ends.
Arrange in a baking dish, sprinkle with the remaining Parmesan and bake for 15 minutes.
Finish under the broiler for 3 minutes to brown the top. The parcels can be served on a bed of fried artichokes, if desired.

Preparation time **40 minuti**
Cooking time **20 minuti**
Level **easy**
Wine **Erbaluce di Caluso**

crunchy lasagna with leeks and matsutake mushrooms

Ingredients for 4 servings

Lasagna:

4 tbsps extra-virgin olive oil

1 leek, thinly sliced

1/2 cup (120 ml) vegetable broth

6 large matsutake mushrooms (see note), about 1 lb (450 g)

1 garlic clove, unpeeled and smashed

5½ oz (150 g) goat's milk cheese

7 tbsps heavy cream, salt and pepper

10 pre-cooked egg lasagna sheets

Preheat the oven to 375°F (190°C or Gas Mark 5).
Heat 2 tablespoons olive oil in a saucepan and sauté the leek over low heat for 10 minutes, gradually adding the vegetable broth.
Clean the mushrooms with damp paper towels moistened with warm water and remove the earthy part of the stalk. Cut them into cubes.
Heat 1 tablespoon olive oil in a non-stick frying pan with the garlic clove.
Add the mushrooms and sauté over high heat.
Mix together the mushrooms, leeks, goat's cheese and cream and adjust salt and pepper. Make alternating layers of the lasagna sheets and mushroom mixture in a baking dish.
Press down well and brush the top with olive oil.
Bake for about 25 minutes, until the surface is browned and crunchy.

Matsutake mushrooms, also known as pine mushrooms, are wild mushrooms which grow in Japan and a few other places around the world. They are prized for their spicy aroma. In this recipe they can be replaced by the same quantity of white mushrooms or a mix of other wild mushrooms.

Preparation time **20 minutes**
Cooking time **40 minutes**
Level **easy**
Wine **Val Venosta Riesling**

leek and asiago lasagna

Ingredients for 4 servings

Lasagna:

1 tab of butter

1 tbsp extra-virgin olive oil

1 leek, sliced, salt

1¼ lb (550 g) fresh egg pasta sheets

2 tbsps grated Parmesan

Béchamel:

2 cups (500 ml) milk

3 tbsps (1½ oz or 40 g) butter

5 tbsps all-purpose flour

nutmeg, salt

9 oz (250 g) Asiago cheese, grated

All forms of Asiago cheese are numbered, and from the number one can tell the date of production and information about how it was produced, down to the names of the farmers who supplied the milk. In this recipe the Asiago can be replaced with Parmesan cheese.

Preheat the oven to 375°F (190°C or Gas Mark 5).
Heat the butter and olive oil in a frying pan and add the leek. Sauté over low heat until soft. Season with salt.
Heat the milk for the béchamel in a saucepan.
In another saucepan melt the butter and mix in the flour.
Cook until the flour begins to brown and then whisk the flour and butter into the boiling milk.
Continue mixing until the béchamel thickens. Season with freshly grated nutmeg and salt.
Pour into a bowl and let cool slightly.
Add the Asiago and stir until cheese melts.
Bring a large pot of salted water to a boil and cook the pasta sheets for 1 minute. Drain and place the pasta on a clean kitchen towel to dry.
Butter a baking dish and layer in the pasta, leeks and béchamel. Add a final layer of leeks and sprinkle with Parmesan. Bake for 20 minutes and serve.

Preparation time **30 minutes**
Cooking time **25 minutes**
Level **medium**
Wine **Bardolino Chiaretto**

summer vegetable lasagna

Ingredients for 4 servings

Pasta dough:

2⅓ cups plus 1 tbsp
(10½ oz or 300 g) all-purpose flour

1 tbsp extra-virgin olive oil

3 eggs, salt

Filling:

4 tbsps extra-virgin olive oil

2 onions, thinly sliced

2 large eggplants, sliced

salt and pepper

8 firm, ripe tomatoes, thickly sliced

1 bunch of basil, **2** tbsps melted butter

4 tbsps grated Parmesan

7 oz (200 g) fresh goat's
cheese, chopped

Did you know that until not that long
ago, giving a pot of basil to a girl
in southern Italy was a way of asking
for her hand in marriage?

Preheat the oven to 400°F (200°C or Gas Mark 6).
Mix together the pasta dough ingredients to form
a smooth, uniform dough. Cover with plastic wrap
and refrigerate for about 30 minutes.
Heat 2 tablespoons olive oil in a frying pan and sauté the
onions with a little water so they soften without coloring.
Heat the remaining 2 tablespoons oil in another frying pan
and sauté the eggplant slices with pinches of salt and
pepper. Grill the tomato slices on a cast-iron grill pan.
Bring a large pot of salted water to a boil.
Roll the dough out into thin sheets and cut into rectangles.
Boil for 3 minutes, then drain and cool under cold, running
water. Pat dry with a clean kitchen towel.
Oil a baking dish. Start with a layer of pasta, then top
it with some eggplant, basil leaves, Parmesan, onions,
tomatoes and goat's cheese and top with another layer
of pasta. Continue until all the ingredients have been used
up, finishing with a layer of pasta. Brush with melted
butter and sprinkle with Parmesan. Bake for 10 minutes.
Let cool slightly before serving.

Preparation time **45 minuti**
Cooking time **20 minuti**
Level **media**
Wine **Etna Bianco**

pea crêpes

Ingredients for 4 servings

Crêpes:

2 eggs, **2** cups (500 ml) milk

3½ oz (100 g) farro or whole-wheat flour

3/4 cup (3½ oz or 100 g) all-purpose flour

salt and white pepper

extra-virgin olive oil

Filling:

2 tbsps extra-virgin olive oil

2 tbsps heavy cream, **1** shallot, minced

2¾ cups (12 oz or 350 g) peas

1/2 cup (120 ml) vegetable broth

2 oz (60 g) mimolette cheese
or other aged, hard cheese, grated

Preheat the oven to 400°F (200°C or Gas Mark 6).
Mix the eggs and milk in a bowl and sift in the flours.
Mix a batter, season with salt and white pepper and let
rest for 20 minutes. Pass the batter through a sieve.
Heat the olive oil for the filling in a frying pan and sauté
the shallot. Add the peas and cover with broth.
Cook over low heat for 15 minutes, then puree in a food
processor with the cream.
The puree should be quite thick.
Heat a non-stick pan with a little olive oil, then make
crêpes, using 1 ladleful of batter at a time.
Let them cool, then spread 1 tablespoon of pea puree
on each one and roll up. Place in a baking dish and cover
with aluminum foil. Bake for 5 minutes, then slice
and serve with the grated cheese.

Baked Pasta

308

⌐ Farro is a type of wheat, also known
as emmer, rich in protein, minerals,
vitamins and fiber. It is currently enjoying a
renaissance in Mediterranean cooking,
but has been used since ancient times.

Preparation time **15 minutes**
Cooking time **30 minutes**
Level **medium**
Wine **Bianco d'Alcamo**

cheesy penne and mushroom timballe

Ingredients for 4 servings

Timballe:

2 oz (50 g) Emmental cheese

2 oz (50 g) mild provolone cheese

1 oz (30 g) Gorgonzola cheese

6 fresh sage leaves, chopped

fresh oregano and marjoram

3½ oz (100 g) ricotta, salt and pepper

10 fresh basil leaves, minced

3 fresh porcini mushrooms

11½ oz (320 g) ridged penne

4 tbsps grated Parmesan cheese

3 tbsps (1½ oz or 40 g) melted butter

Provolone was traditionally a southern Italian cheese, but has also been made in the north since 1824. As often happens in such cases, as with mozzarella, the use of milk from the Po Valley gives the northern cheese a lighter, milder taste than the southern version.

Preheat the oven to 450°F (230°C or Gas Mark 8).
Puree the Emmental, provolone and Gorgonzola together with the sage, oregano and a little marjoram in a food processor.
Mix the ricotta and basil together.
Clean the porcini, removing the earthy part of the stalk and wiping them with a damp paper towel. Slice them.
Bring a large pot of salted water to a boil and cook the penne until al dente. Drain and toss with the ricotta mixture, mushrooms and grated Parmesan.
Season with salt and pepper
Line an oval baking dish with parchment paper, leaving large borders so that the paper can be closed over the top. Brush the paper with butter, then spread a layer of the penne mixture in the bottom. Top with half of the cheese puree, then with the remaining pasta. Finish with a layer of cheese and the remaining melted butter. Close the paper over the top and bake for about 5 minutes. Serve, opening the paper only at the table.

Preparation time **20 minutes**
Cooking time **20 minutes**
Level **easy**
Wine **Nero d'Avola**

baked tagliolini with porcini ragù

Ingredients for 4 servings

Pasta dough:

2⅓ cups plus 1 tbsp
(10½ oz or 300 g) all-purpose flour

3 eggs

1 tbsp extra-virgin olive oil, salt

Ragù:

4 tbsps extra-virgin olive oil

1 shallot, minced, **2** garlic cloves

4 fresh porcini mushrooms,
thinly sliced

salt and pepper

3 tbsps grated Parmesan

2 tbsps (1 oz or 30 g) melted butter

Preheat the oven to 350°F (180°C or Gas Mark 4).
Mix together the flour, eggs, olive oil and a pinch of salt.
Knead to form a smooth and elastic dough.
Roll the dough into a ball, wrap in plastic wrap and
refrigerate for 20 minutes.
Heat 2 tablespoons olive oil with the shallot and garlic
and sauté the mushrooms until soft.
Season with salt and pepper.
Roll out the pasta into thin sheets. Roll up the pasta
and slice thinly to form tagliolini. Dust a wooden cutting
board with flour and toss the tagliolini in the flour.
Let the pasta dry. Bring a large pot of salted water
to a boil. Boil the tagliolini for a few minutes and drain.
Drizzle 2 tablespoons of olive oil over the pasta.
Butter a soufflé dish. Pour in half the tagliolini and top
with half the mushroom ragù, 1 tablespoon Parmesan
and 1 tablespoon butter. Mix to combine and form
a second layer with the remaining pasta, ragù, butter
and Parmesan. Bake for 15 minutes.

Fresh porcini mushrooms should
be eaten as soon as possible
after picking to best enjoy
their flavor and fragrance.

Preparation time **20 minutes**
Cooking time **40 minutes**
Level **easy**
Wine **Lago di Caldaro Schiava**

baked tuscan-style macaroni

Ingredients for 8 servings
Macaroni:

2 tbsps extra-virgin olive oil

1 onion, minced

1 carrot, minced

1 celery stalk, minced

3½ oz (100 g) prosciutto, diced

salt and pepper, nutmeg

3 tomatoes, diced, beef broth

1 goose, cut into small pieces

1⅓ lb (600 g) macaroni
or rigatoni pasta

grated Parmesan cheese

1 tbsp breadcrumbs

3½ tbsps (2 oz or 50 g)
butter, chopped

Heat the olive oil in a large saucepan and sauté the onion, carrot and celery. Add the prosciutto, salt, pepper and freshly grated nutmeg and continue cooking for 10 minutes over medium heat.
Add the tomatoes and a ladleful of broth. Continue cooking for about 1 hour, gradually adding more broth.
Add the goose to the sauce and cook for 10 minutes.
Preheat the oven to 485°F (250°C or Gas Mark 10).
Bring a large pot of salted water to a boil and cook the pasta until al dente. Drain and toss with the sauce.
Butter a baking dish. Pour in a layer of pasta, top with Parmesan and add another layer of pasta.
Continue, finishing with a layer of Parmesan.
Sprinkle over the breadcrumbs and top with pieces of butter. Bake for 5 minutes. Serve hot.

Preparation time **20 minutes**
Cooking time **1 hour 30 minutes**
Level **medium**
Wine **Morellino di Scansano**

potato and taleggio lasagna

Ingredients for 4 servings

Lasagna:

2 white-fleshed potatoes (about 10½ oz or 300 g)

2 tbsp extra-virgin olive oil

1 garlic clove, smashed

5-6 mushrooms, plus extra for garnish, peeled and sliced, salt and pepper

7 oz (200 g) spinach, nutmeg

1¼ cups (300 ml) milk, parsley, minced

7 oz (200 g) Taleggio cheese, chopped

14 oz (400 g) fresh lasagna sheets

3½ tbsps (2 oz or 50 g) butter, chopped

3 tbsps grated Parmesan cheese

Garnish:

mushrooms, halved (optional)

Taleggio is a creamy cow's milk cheese with a nutty flavor from Lombardy. In this recipe it can be replaced with another melting cheese, such as fontina.

Preheat the oven to 400°F (200°C or Gas Mark 6). Boil the potatoes until just tender, then drain, peel and mash in a bowl. Peel the mushrooms and slice them. Heat 1 tablespoon olive oil with the garlic and sauté the mushrooms, seasoning with salt, pepper and parsley. Heat 1 tablespoon olive oil in another frying pan and sauté the spinach, seasoning it with salt and freshly grated nutmeg. Bring the milk to a boil and add the mashed potatoes. Stir until smooth, then add the Taleggio and stir until melted. Keep warm.

Bring a large pot of salted water to a boil and cook the lasagna sheets for 1 minute. Drain and immerse in cold water, then drain and let dry on a clean kitchen towel. Butter a baking dish and make layers of the pasta sheets, the potato puree, the mushrooms and the spinach. Finish with a sprinkling of Parmesan and pieces of butter. Bake for 30 minutes. Serve, garnished with mushroom halves if desired.

Preparation time **25 minutes**
Cooking time **1 hour**
Level **easy**
Wine **Friuli Collio Merlot**

gratinéed cannelloni
with savoy cabbage and provola

Ingredients for 8 servings
Cannelloni:

6 tbsps extra-virgin olive oil

2 garlic cloves, smashed

1/2 head of Savoy cabbage, shredded

1/2 cup (120 ml) vegetable broth

1/2 cup (120 ml) white wine

salt and pepper

12 dried cannelloni tubes

7 oz (200 g) smoked provola or
other smoked cheese, diced

1 tomato, diced

Bêchamel:

1 tab of butter

3 tbsps all-purpose flour

1 cup (250 ml) hot milk

salt

Preheat the oven to 400°F (200°C or Gas Mark 6).
Heat half the olive oil in a saucepan with the garlic cloves
and add the cabbage. Season with salt and add a little
vegetable broth and the wine. Let cook for 7-8 minutes
over high heat, seasoning with salt and pepper to taste.
Remove from the heat and let cool.
Meanwhile bring a large pot of salted water to a boil
and blanch the cannelloni, then drain and immerse in cold
water to cool. Drain and halve them, and arrange them
standing up in an oiled baking dish.
Mix the cabbage and provola together and fill the
cannelloni with the mixture.
Top with some pieces of tomato. Bake for 25 minutes.
Meanwhile melt the butter and stir in the flour. Whisk
in the hot milk and a pinch of salt and cook until
thickened. Serve the cannelloni hot, accompanied
by the béchamel.

Preparation time **20 minutes**
Cooking time **40 minutes**
Level **easy**
Wine **Friuli Collio Sauvignon**

cold pasta

cold sardinian gnocchetti with zucchini and cherry tomatoes

Ingredients for 4 servings

Gnocchetti:

2 tbsps extra-virgin olive oil

1 garlic clove, smashed

3 baby zucchini, thickly sliced

salt and pepper

1/2 cup (120 ml) vegetable broth

12½ oz (350 g) Sardinian gnocchetti or other short pasta

3-4 basil leaves

7-8 cherry tomatoes, quartered

1 tbsp pine nuts, toasted and chopped

Heat the olive oil in a frying pan and sauté the garlic. Add the zucchini, season with salt and pepper and brown slightly. Add the broth, cover and cook until tender. Meanwhile bring a large pot of salted water to a boil and cook the gnocchetti until al dente.
Drain and cool under cold running water.
Let the cooked zucchini cool, then discard the garlic and puree the zucchini in a food processor with the basil. Stir the gnocchetti into the zucchini sauce together with the cherry tomatoes and pine nuts. Serve.

Choose zucchini which are firm, with a tight, shiny skin. The smaller, thinner zucchini have fewer seeds, and should be covered with a light down.

Preparation time **20 minutes**
Cooking time **15 minutes**
Level **easy**
Wine **Torbato di Alghero**

cold orecchiette with vegetable caponata

Ingredients for 4 servings

Orecchiette:

3 tbsps extra-virgin olive oil

1 yellow onion, minced

1 garlic clove, smashed

1/2 eggplant, deseeded and diced

5-6 asparagus spears, sliced

2 carrots, diced, salt and pepper

2 zucchini, green part only, diced

hot vegetable broth (optional)

3 basil leaves

12½ oz (350 g) orecchiette
or other short pasta

1 tomato, deseeded and diced

Heat the olive oil and sauté the onion until golden.
Add the garlic and eggplant, then the asparagus.
Cook for 3 minutes, then add the carrots.
Season with salt and pepper. Add the zucchini together
with a little broth or hot water and basil.
Bring a pot of salted water to a boil and add the
orecchiette. As soon as they are al dente drain and cool
under cold running water. Once the vegetables are cooked,
remove from the heat and let cool.
Add tomatoes and pasta, let rest 20 minutes, then serve.

When buying asparagus, make sure the
tips are fresh-looking, tightly closed,
straight and without dark marks.
The stalks should not be too woody.

Preparation time **20 minutes**
Cooking time **20 minutes**
Level **easy**
Wine **Bianco d'Alcamo**

pasta salad with tomatoes, peppers and cucumbers

Ingredients for 4 servings

Pasta salad:

salt and pepper

14 oz (400 g) pasta wheels (ruote)

1 tomato, chopped

1/4 red bell pepper, chopped

1 carrot, peeled and chopped

1/2 cucumber, peeled and chopped

1 celery stalk, fibers removed, chopped

2 spring onions, sliced

4 tbsps extra-virgin olive oil

grated Parmesan cheese (optional)

For an even smoother sauce, after pureeing the vegetables pass the puree through a wide-mesh sieve to eliminate any fibers or bits of skin.

Bring a large pot of salted water to a boil and cook the pasta wheels until al dente.
Drain and cool under cold running water.
Place the tomato, bell pepper, carrot, cucumber, celery and 1 spring onion in a food processor with the olive oil, salt and pepper and puree until smooth.
Pour the vegetable puree over the pasta and mix well.
Let sit for 10 minutes, then serve, garnished with the remaining spring onion.
Sprinkle with grated Parmesan if desired.

Preparation time **10 minutes**
Cooking time **10 minutes**
Level **easy**
Wine **Sicilia Chardonnay**

cold lime spaghetti with lumpfish roe

Ingredients for 4 servings
Spaghetti:

12½ oz (350 g) spaghetti
2 tbsps extra-virgin olive oil
1 tbsp red lumpfish roe
1 tbsp black lumpfish roe
grated zest of 1 lime
parsley, minced
1 tbsp trout roe

Bring a large pot of salted water to a boil and cook the spaghetti until al dente. Drain and place in a bowl. Toss with the olive oil, red and black lumpfish roe, grated lime zest and a little minced parsley and continue mixing until evenly combined.
Take a quarter of the spaghetti and form it into a nest in the center of an individual serving plate or bowl. Continue with the other three portions, then top each with a little trout roe and serve.

Lumpfish roe is available preserved in salt or tinned, and after caviar is one of the fish roes most commonly used in the kitchen.

Preparation time **10 minutes**
Cooking time **10 minutes**
Level **easy**
Wine **Trentino Nosiola**

gnocchi with smoked salmon and fennel

Ingredients for 4 servings

Gnocchi:

salt and pepper

14 oz (400 g) semolina gnocchi
or other short pasta

1 fennel bulb

juice of 1/2 lemon

2 young zucchini with flowers
attached, thinly sliced

7 oz (200 g) smoked salmon,
cut into strips

1 bunch wild fennel or dill, minced

3 tbsps extra-virgin olive oil

Bring a pot of salted water to a boil and cook the gnocchi until al dente. Drain and cool under running water.
Boil the fennel in water and lemon juice until tender. Drain, cool and slice thinly.
Mix with the zucchini, salmon, wild fennel and olive oil and season with salt and pepper.
Toss the gnocchi with the sauce, let sit for a few minutes then serve.

Excellent smoked salmon can be found in supermarkets and specialty stores, usually from Norway or Scotland. Always check the expiration date, that the fish is a uniform pinkish orange color and that there are no dried-out edges or beads of moisture.

Preparation time **15 minutes**
Cooking time **20 minutes**
Level **easy**
Wine **Bolgheri Bianco**

ziti salad with tuna and tomato

Ingredients for 4 servings
Ziti:

salt and pepper

10½ oz (300 g) ziti-type pasta

1 tomato, cut into thin wedges

1 bag of chopped mixed lettuces

(butter,lettuce, frisée, radicchio, romaine)

1 tsp oregano

7 oz (200 g) tuna fillet in oil, drained

3 tbsps extra-virgin olive oil

Bring a large pot of salted water to a boil and cook the ziti until just al dente.
Drain and cool under running water. Cut the ziti into 1 1/2-inch (4 cm) lengths and place in a bowl.
Mix in the tomato, lettuces and oregano.
Arrange on a serving plate and crumble over the tuna.
Dress with olive oil, salt and pepper and serve.

332

Tuna is high in fat but also in protein and minerals, and is considered a healthy, energy-giving food. It can be found in cans and jars, packed in brine, vegetable oil or olive oil.

Preparation time **15 minutes**
Cooking time **10 minutes**
Level **easy**
Wine **Ciró Bianco**

fusilli, tuna and summer vegetable salad

Ingredients for 4 servings
Fusilli:

5 baby zucchini

salt and pepper

10½ oz (300 g) fusilli

4 tbsps extra-virgin olive oil

fresh basil leaves, minced
and whole for garnish

2 oz (60 g) smoked provola or other
mild smoked cheese, diced

1 tin of tuna in oil, drained
and crumbled

1 bunch of arugula, **6** cherry tomatoes

3 tbsps pitted black olives, chopped

Slice the zucchini lengthwise into quarters. Heat a cast-iron grill pan and grill the zucchini slices. Season with salt.
Bring a large pot of salted water to a boil and cook the fusilli until still very al dente.
Drain and run under cold water for 3-4 minutes to cool, then transfer to a large bowl.
Toss with olive oil, minced basil, salt and pepper.
Add the cheese, tuna, arugula, tomatoes, grilled zucchini and olives and stir. Let sit for 20 minutes, then serve garnished with basil leaves.

For a more intense flavor, replace the tuna with mackerel fillets in oil, and use thyme instead of basil.

Preparation time **25 minutes**
Cooking time **12 minutes**
Level **easy**
Wine **Bianco Capena**

cold tortiglioni with peas
and roast pepper

Ingredients for 4 servings
Tortiglioni:

1 red bell pepper

2 tbsps extra-virgin olive oil

1 shallot, minced

1/2 cup (120 ml) vegetable broth

1 cup (4 oz or 120 g) spring peas

2 carrots, diced

3 tbsps heavy cream

lemon thyme, salt and pepper

14 oz (400 g) tortiglioni, garganelli
or penne pasta

Fruits and vegetables called "spring"
or "baby" are usually tenderer and
sweeter than their larger counterparts,
as their sugars have not yet been
converted into starch. The exact
moment of harvesting can affect the
quality, and a delay of even just a
few days can have a significant impact.

Preheat the oven to 475°F (240°C or Gas Mark 9).
Cut the pepper in half and remove the seeds and the white pith. Wash under running water, dry well then brush lightly with olive oil and cut into thick strips.
Place on a baking sheet and roast in the oven for 10 minutes. Remove from the oven, place in a plastic bag and let steam for 15 minutes.
Peel, cut into strips and set aside.
Heat 1 tablespoon olive oil and sauté the shallot. Add the vegetable broth, peas and carrot. Cook for 10 minutes, then remove from the heat and let cool.
Add the roasted bell pepper strips, cream and thyme to the peas and carrots and season with salt and pepper to taste. Bring a large pot of salted water to a boil and cook the pasta until al dente.
Drain and cool under cold running water. Toss with the vegetables, then let sit for 20 minutes before serving.

Preparation time **20 minutes**
Cooking time **20 minutes**
Level **easy**
Wine **Gambellara**

cold pasta shells with grilled vegetables and smoked scamorza

Ingredients for 4 servings

Pasta Shells:

10½ oz (300 g) grilled bell peppers, eggplant and zucchini in oil

10½ oz (300 g) pasta shells

salt

1/4 cup (1 oz or 30 g) pitted black olives

fresh basil or chives

4 miniature smoked scamorza cheeses thinly sliced

2 tbsps extra-virgin olive oil

Drain the grilled vegetables, dice and transfer to a large serving bowl.
Boil the pasta in abundant salted water for the amount of time indicated on the package. Drain and cool under cold running water.
Add the pasta to the vegetables and add the olives, torn basil leaves (or minced chives) and scamorza cheese.
Drizzle over a little olive oil and season with salt.
Mix carefully and let rest for a few minutes before serving.

Try substituting the grilled peppers with thinly sliced radicchio. You can also substitute smoked scamorza with mozzarella.

Preparation time **5 minutes**
Cooking time **10 minutes**
Level **easy**
Wine **Ribolla Gialla**

anelli with olives and tofu sausages

Ingredients for 4 servings

Anelli:

salt and pepper

12½ oz (350 g) anelli pasta
or other pasta rings

3 tbsps extra-virgin olive oil

1 garlic clove, unpeeled and halved

1/2 head of escarole, coarsely chopped

20 black olives

4 tofu sausages, chopped

1 thyme sprig, leaves only

Bring a large pot of salted water to a boil and cook
the pasta until al dente.
Drain and rinse under cold running water to cool.
Heat the olive oil in a frying pan with the garlic.
Add the escarole and a little water if necessary and cook
over low heat until tender.
Remove the garlic and add the olives and tofu sausages.
Let cook for 10 minutes, then let cool.
Mix the pasta with the sauce, adjust salt and pepper
and stir in the thyme. Serve cold.

The tofu could be replaced
with cheese, such as
Swiss Emmental.

Preparation time **20 minutes**
Cooking time **20 minutes**
Level **easy**
Wine **Blanc de Morgex et de La Salle**

rice sedanini with tomatoes and arugula pesto

Ingredients for 4 servings

Sedanini:

3 firm tomatoes, salt and pepper

14 oz (400 g) rice sedanini or other short rice pasta

4 tbsps extra-virgin olive oil

10 black olives, pitted and chopped

Pesto:

1 bunch of arugula, **5** basil leaves

4 tbsps extra-virgin olive oil

1 tbsp grated Parmesan cheese

1 tbsp pine nuts, salt and pepper

Bring a large pot of salted water to a boil and cook the sedanini until al dente.
Drain and cool under cold running water to stop them overcooking. Transfer to a bowl and toss with a little olive oil to prevent sticking.
Blanch the tomatoes in boiling water, drain and let cool. Peel, deseed and dice.
Toss with a little salt and pepper and stir in the olives. Mix together the pasta and tomato mixture and add the rest of the olive oil.
Puree all the pesto ingredients in a food processor. Serve the pasta drizzled with the pesto.

342

Arugula was a favorite on the tables of Ancient Rome, and the poets Horace and Martial both talked of it. The plant can reach up to 1/2 feet (50 cm) high, and the more arid the ground the spicier the leaves will be.

Preparation time **15 minutes**
Cooking time **10 minutes**
Level **easy**
Wine **Cinque Terre**

riccioli, radicchio and chicken sausage salad

Ingredients for 4 servings
Riccioli:

salt and pepper

10½ oz (300 g) riccioli or fusilli

2 tbsps extra-virgin olive oil

1 garlic clove, smashed

1 head of radicchio, preferably Treviso, shredded

5½ oz (150 g) fresh ricotta

4 oz (120 g) chicken sausage, cooked and chopped

Bring a large pot of salted water to a boil and cook the pasta until al dente. Drain and cool under cold running water. Heat a non-stick frying pan with 1 tablespoon olive oil and garlic. Add the radicchio and briefly sauté, seasoning with salt and pepper.
Beat the ricotta to a cream with the remaining tablespoon of olive oil and season with salt and pepper.
Mix together the pasta, chicken sausage, radicchio and ricotta. Adjust salt and pepper and serve the salad in small individual serving bowls.

If you have any of this salad left over, it can be turned into a hot dish by placing it in a baking dish, topping it with pieces of fontina and broiling it. The chicken sausage makes the dish lighter, but it could be replaced with pork sausage or eliminated all together for a vegetarian dish.

Preparation time **10 minutes**
Cooking time **12 minutes**
Level **easy**
Wine **Cirò Rosato**

farro and corn fusilli with vegetable ratatouille

Ingredients for 4 servings
Fusilli:

2 tbsps extra-virgin olive oil

1 onion, minced

2 celery stalks, diced

2 zucchini, diced

1/2 white turnip, diced

1 carrot, diced, salt and pepper

5 basil leaves, torn

5½ oz (150 g) aged ricotta

6 oz (170 g) farro or whole-wheat fusilli

6 oz (170 g) corn fusilli

2 tbsps sliced almonds, toasted

Heat the olive oil in a large frying pan and sauté the onion.
Add the celery, carrot, zucchini and turnip and
1 tablespoon water and let cook until tender.
Season with salt and pepper to taste. Stir in the basil.
Beat the ricotta in a bowl with the tines of a fork,
adding a little hot water, until it forms a soft cream.
Bring a large pot of salted water to a boil and cook
the two kinds of fusilli until al dente.
Drain and toss with the vegetables and ricotta. Let cool,
then garnish with toasted almonds before serving.

Nuts nutritionally complement
pasta, making for a complete
meal with balanced protein,
minerals and fat.

Preparation time **15 minutes**
Cooking time **25 minutes**
Level **easy**
Wine **Roero Arneis**

spaghetti with ginger oil and caviar

Ingredients for 4 servings
Spaghetti:

4 tbsps extra-virgin olive oil
fresh ginger, thinly sliced
coarse salt
7 oz (200 g) spaghetti
1½ oz (40 g) Sevruga caviar
chives
sour cream (optional)

Infuse the olive oil with the ginger slices, then strain the oil. Bring a large pot of salted water to a boil and cook the spaghetti until al dente, then drain and cool in ice water. Drain again and dry on a clean kitchen towel. Place in a bowl and toss with the ginger oil, stirring with a fork.
Arrange the spaghetti on serving plates either laid out flat or in nests. Either dot the caviar on the flat spaghetti or form it into quenelles with two teaspoons and use it to top the nests.
Garnish with chives and if desired, some sour cream.

The term "quenelle" is a French word, and refers to ingredients shaped between two spoons or with the hands into an elongated, oval shape.

Preparation time **10 minutes**
Cooking time **7 minutes**
Level **easy**
Wine **Bolgheri Bianco**

cold paccheri with sea bream tartar and caviar

Ingredients for 4 servings
Paccheri:

salt and white pepper

12 Gragnano paccheri (see note)

10½ oz (300 g) sea bream fillet, deboned and finely minced

2 tsps lemon juice

3 tbsps light extra-virgin olive oil

1/2 spring onion, finely minced

chives, finely minced

2 oz (50 g) Osetra caviar

1 red chile pepper, thinly sliced into rings (optional)

Paccheri are typical to the region of Campania, traditionally from the small pasta-making town of Gragnano. They were once known as "the pasta of the poor" because it takes just a few to fill up a plate. In this recipe they could be replaced by cannelloni.

Bring a large pot of salted water to a boil and cook the paccheri until al dente.
Drain and immerse in ice water. Drain again and pat dry.
Dress the fish with lemon juice, salt, white pepper, olive oil, spring onion and chives.
Use the mixture to fill the paccheri.
Top the paccheri with a little caviar.
If desired, garnish with rings of red chili pepper.

Preparation time **10 minutes**
Cooking time **12 minutes**
Level **easy**
Wine **Trebbiano d'Abruzzo**

stuffed tomatoes

Ingredients for 4 servings

Cold Pasta:

4 large, ripe tomatoes

salt and pepper

3 tbsps extra-virgin olive oil

1 shallot, minced

1/3 cup (2 oz or 50 g) spring peas

1 carrot, diced, **1** egg

8 oz (220 g) egg pasta fiocchetti or other small pasta

4 mushrooms, thinly sliced

grated zest of 1 organic lime

chives, minced

The tomatoes could be filled with cooked rice and accompanied by diced marinated tofu. Make the marinade by whisking together soy sauce, sesame oil and a little minced garlic. For a stronger flavor, add 1 tsp mild mustard and some freshly grated ginger as well.

Slice the top off the tomatoes to make lids. Scoop out the flesh, salt the inside and turn them upside-down in a colander for 20 minutes to drain. Meanwhile heat the olive oil and sauté the shallot together with a spoonful of water until soft. Remove from the heat and let cool.

Blanch the peas and diced carrot in boiling water until tender. Beat the egg with a pinch of salt. Make an omelet in a small non-stick frying pan, then remove from the pan and thinly slice.

Bring a large pot of salted water to a boil and cook the pasta. Drain and cool under cold running water. Mix with the shallot and let rest for 20 minutes. Mix together the pasta, mushrooms, peas, carrots and omelet. Season with grated lime zest and chives. Fill the tomatoes with the mixture and serve.

Preparation time **20 minutes**
Cooking time **40 minutes**
Level **easy**
Wine **Bianco d'Alcamo**

farfalle with shrimp and arugula pesto

Ingredients for 4 servings

Farfalle:

1 bunch (about 5½ oz or 150 g) arugula,
plus extra for garnish

1 garlic clove

3 tbsps grated Parmesan cheese,
plus extra for garnish

6 tbsps extra-virgin olive oil

salt and pepper

7 oz (200 g) shrimp, shelled,
deveined and diced

1/3 cup (2 oz or 50 g) pine nuts

5 cherry tomatoes, quartered

14 oz (400 g) farfalle pasta

Blend the arugula, garlic clove and Parmesan in a food processor. Drizzle in the olive oil and pulse to combine. Season to taste with salt and pepper.

Heat the remaining olive oil in a frying pan and add the shrimp. Sauté for a few minutes, then season to taste with salt and pepper.

Toast the pine nuts under the broiler until golden brown. Remove from the oven and add to the shrimp.

Add the pesto and cherry tomatoes to the shrimp mixture and stir to combine.

Boil the pasta in abundant salted water until al dente. Drain and cool under cold running water.

Transfer Pasta to the pan with the sauce.

Serve the pasta topped with a grating of Parmesan and garnished with arugula leaves.

For a creamier sauce, add 1 tablespoon of ricotta to the arugula pesto and stir with a wooden spoon until smooth.

Preparation time **25 minutes**
Cooking time **35 minutes**
Level **easy**
Wine **Riesling dell'Oltrepò Pavese**

soups

Pasta

spicy tomato broth with shrimp ravioli

Ingredients for 4 servings
Broth:

6 tomatoes, **2** shallots, minced
2 tbsps extra-virgin olive oil
1 dried red chili pepper, **1** star anise
chicken or vegetable broth
salt and pepper

Pasta:

16 jumbo shrimp, shelled,
deveined and diced
1 tbsp extra-virgin olive oil
salt and pepper
1/2 bunch of fresh dill, minced
7 oz (200 g) fresh egg pasta sheets

Garnish:

1 tbsp extra-virgin olive oil
1/4 pineapple, peeled and cubed
4 mushrooms, dill sprigs

Sauté means to cook over fairly high heat, usually with the addition of a fat such as olive oil. Adding liquid can help slow down the cooking speed.

Preheat the oven to 350°F (180°C or Gas Mark 4).
Halve the tomatoes and arrange on a baking tray.
Drizzle with 1 tablespoon olive oil and roast in the oven for 25-30 minutes. Mix the diced shrimp with the olive oil, salt, pepper and minced dill. Mix well.
Place spoonfuls of the mixture on half of the pasta sheets. Top with the other half of the sheets and cut out ravioli using a ravioli cutter or a rolling cutter.
Place the shallots, chili, star anise and 1 tablespoon olive oil in a saucepan. Gently sauté, then add the roasted tomatoes and bring to a simmer. Cover with broth and bring to a boil. Adjust salt and pepper, then puree the mixture and pass it through a sieve.
Heat 1 tablespoon olive oil in a non-stick sauté pan, then add the pineapple and mushrooms and sauté for a few minutes, seasoning with salt and pepper. Bring a large pot of salted water to a boil and cook the ravioli until done. Compose shallow soup bowls with a ladleful of tomato broth, 3-4 ravioli, pineapple and mushrooms and garnish with dill sprigs.

Preparation time **30 minutes**
Cooking time **55 minutes**
Level **medium**
Wine **Friuli Collio Sauvignon**

porcini cappelletti in truffle broth

Ingredients for 4 servings
Pasta dough:
1¾ cups (8 oz or 220 g) all-purpose flour
2 eggs, salt
Filling:
3 fresh porcini mushrooms
2 tbsps extra-virgin olive oil
1 shallot, minced, thyme leaves
1 egg, beaten, salt and pepper
1 tbsp breadcrumbs
1 tbsp grated Parmesan cheese
Broth:
2 cups (500 ml) chicken broth
1 small truffle, shaved
Garnish:
mint (optional)

Before cutting out the cappelletti, make sure there is no air trapped between the pasta sheets by pressing down firmly around the filling with the fingertips, and sprinkle the dough with flour so the cutter doesn't stick to it.

Mix together the flour, eggs and a little salt to make a smooth dough, adding water as necessary.
Wrap in plastic wrap and refrigerate for 30 minutes.
Meanwhile clean the porcini and trim off the earthy part of the stalk. Dice them.
Heat the olive oil in a frying pan and sauté the shallot.
Add the porcini and sauté. Add the thyme, salt and pepper.
Once cooked, add a little hot water and let cool.
Puree the cooled mushrooms in a food processor and stir in the egg, breadcrumbs and Parmesan.
Roll the pasta dough out into 2 thin sheets. Place small mounds (about 1/2 teaspoon each) of the porcini mixture on a sheet and cover with the other one.
Cut out the cappelletti with a small round cookie cutter.
Bring the chicken broth to a boil with the truffle shavings and cook the cappelletti.
Serve hot, sprinkled with mint leaves if desired.

Preparation time **40 minutes**
Cooking time **25 minutes**
Level **easy**
Wine **Gutturnio Classico**

cappelletti in chicken broth

Ingredients for 4 servings
Broth:
1/2 free-range chicken
1 onion, chopped, **2** carrots, chopped
2 celery stalks, chopped
1 tomato, quartered
Pasta dough:
2⅓ cups plus 1 tbsp (10½ oz or 300 g) all-purpose flour
2 eggs, **2** egg yolks
salt
Filling:
9 oz (250 g) braised or roast beef or veal, with its cooking juices and vegetables
5½ oz (150 g) ricotta
1 tbsp grated Parmesan cheese
salt and pepper, nutmeg
Garnish:
Parmesan cheese, shaved (optional)

Place the chicken, onion, carrots, celery and tomato in a large saucepan and cover with cold water. Bring to a boil and simmer for 1 hour 30 minutes from the moment the water starts boiling. Let cool, then strain the broth. Meanwhile mix together the pasta dough ingredients until smooth. Wrap in plastic wrap and let rest in the refrigerator for 30 minutes. Blend the braised or roast beef or veal and vegetables in a food processor, then stir in the ricotta and Parmesan cheese. Add salt, pepper and freshly grated nutmeg to taste. Roll the pasta dough out thinly. Use a round cookie cutter to cut out circles of dough, 2 inches (5 cm) in diameter. Place a teaspoonful of the filling in the middle of each circle and fold them over to make half-moons. Wrap the half-moons around the little finger, giving them a half twist so that a pair of corners turns up and pressing the other pair together to make little rings. Bring half the chicken broth to a boil and cook the cappelletti. Meanwhile heat the other half in a separate pan. Drain the cappelletti and transfer them to shallow soup bowls, then cover with the fresh broth. Serve sprinkled with Parmesan shavings, if desired.

Preparation time **30 minutes**
Cooking time **1 hour 30 minutes**
Level **easy**
Wine **Lambrusco di Sorbara**

goulash with egg noodles

Ingredients for 4 servings

Goulash:

3 tbsps extra-virgin olive oil

1 onion, minced

2 oz (50 g) smoked pancetta
or bacon, diced

vegetable broth (optional)

1 tsp strong paprika, **2** tsps mild paprika

1/2 tsp ground cumin

1⅓ lb (600 g) beef, cubed

1 tbsp all-purpose flour

1 potato, peeled and diced

1/2 bell pepper, diced, salt and pepper

10½ oz (300 g) egg noodles

Heat 2 tablespoons olive oil in a large saucepan and sauté the onion and pancetta or bacon. Add a little broth or water and cook gently until the onion is softened. Remove from the heat and add the different kinds of paprika and the cumin. Return to the heat and add a drop of water. Add the beef and brown over high heat. Sprinkle with the flour and pour over more broth or water. Continue cooking.
Meanwhile heat 1 tablespoon olive oil in a frying pan and sauté the bell pepper.
Add the potato and season with salt and pepper.
Once browned, add the mixture to the meat and let the stew simmer for 10-15 minutes over low heat.
Bring a large pot of salted water to a boil and cook the egg noodles until al dente. Drain and add to the stew.
Let sit for 3 minutes before serving.

64

Goulash is a typical Austro-Hungarian dish which is famous around the world. There are many different variations, but they all contain lots of paprika.

Preparation time **30 minutes**
Cooking time **30 minutes**
Level **easy**
Wine **Refosco dal Peduncolo Rosso**

maltagliati with beans

Ingredients for 4 servings

Pasta dough:

2⅓ cups plus 1 tbsp (10½ oz or 300 g)
all-purpose flour

3 eggs

Sauce:

1/2 cup (60 ml) extra-virgin olive oil

1 garlic clove, mince, **1/2** onion, minced

1 carrot, minced, **1** celery stalk, minced

1¾ lb (800 g) fresh beans
(such as cranberry)

8 cups (2 l) water, rosemary, minced, salt

Garnish:

freshly ground black pepper

grated Parmesan cheese

The fresh beans could be replaced
with 1½ cups (10½ oz or 300 g) dried
beans, soaked overnight.

Mound the flour on a wooden pastry board and make
a well in the center. Break the eggs into the center.
Work the dough by hand until smooth and uniform.
Roll the dough out thinly with a rolling pin, then roll
it up and slice the roll into thick tagliatelle. Using a fluted
rolling cutter, cut the tagliatelle into uneven pieces.
Flour them and lay them out on a tray covered by a clean
kitchen towel. Let rest in a dry place for 2 hours.
Meanwhile heat the olive oil in a frying pan and sauté
the garlic. Add the onion, carrot and celery and sauté until
softened. Add the water, beans and rosemary.
Cook over medium heat, adding extra water if necessary,
until the beans are done. Adjust the salt.
Bring a large pot of salted water to a boil and cook
the maltagliati until al dente. Drain and add to the beans.
Serve with a grinding of black pepper and a sprinkling
of grated Parmesan.

Preparation time **30 minutes**
Cooking time **50 minutes**
Level **medium**
Wine **Colli Bolognesi Merlot**

anolini in broth

Ingredients for 6 servings

Filling:

7 tbsps (3½ oz or 100 g) butter

1 onion, minced, **1** carrot, minced

1 celery stalk, minced, **14** oz (400 g) beef

2 cloves, salt and pepper

4 cups (1 litre) beef broth

1½ cups (350 ml) red wine

1 tbsp ready-made tomato sauce

1½ cups (6½ oz or 180 g) breadcrumbs

1⅔ cups (5½ oz or 160 g) grated Parmesan cheese, plus extra for garnish

4 eggs, beaten, nutmeg

Pasta dough:

4¾ cups (1⅓ lb or 600 g) all-purpose flour

5 eggs, salt

◪ This recipe is traditionally prepared with donkey meat.

Melt the butter in a large saucepan and sauté the onion, carrot and celery. Add the beef, cloves and pepper. Let the meat brown, then cover with beef broth. Continue cooking over low heat for 8-10 hours, adding a little red wine every so often. If the meat starts drying out, add extra broth. About 6-7 hours after starting cooking, add the tomato sauce, mixed first with a little hot water. When the meat starts disintegrating, remove from the heat and let cool. Once cool, finely chop the meat. Mix the breadcrumbs into the remaining cooking liquid and mix together with the meat, Parmesan, eggs and a pinch of freshly grated nutmeg. Add salt and pepper and mix well. Mix together the flour and eggs for the pasta dough together with a pinch of salt, adding more water if necessary to make a smooth dough. Roll out the dough thinly and cut into strips 4 inches (9 cm) wide. Place spoonfuls of the filling mixture along one side of the strips, then fold them over and press down around the filling to expel any air. Cut out anolini using a small fluted rectangular cookie cutter. Bring the beef broth to a boil and cook the anolini. Serve hot with grated Parmesan.

Preparation time **1 hour**
Cooking time **10 hours**
Level **medium**
Wine **Colli di Parma Rosso**

spring vegetable soup with rye pasta

Ingredients for 4 servings
Soup:

4 tbsps extra-virgin olive oil
1 onion, sliced, **2** carrots, diced
1 celery stalk, diced, salt
3/4 cup (3½ oz or 100 g) peas
2/3 cup (3½ oz or 100 g) fava beans
1 tsp tomato concentrate
4 cups (1 litre) water
3 cups (3½ oz or 100 g) shredded
Swiss chard
4 oz (120 g) thin rye tagliatelle
basil, julienned
flakes of nori seaweed, toasted (optional)

Heat 2 tablespoons olive oil in a saucepan and sauté the onion, carrot and celery with a pinch of salt.
Add the peas, favas and tomato concentrate and cover with water. Adjust the salt, bring the water to a boil and cook for 10-15 minutes over moderate heat.
Add the chard, return to a boil and add the tagliatelle. Continue cooking until pasta is done then remove from the heat.
Serve topped with drizzle of olive oil, julienned basil and flakes of toasted nori seaweed, if desired.

Nori seaweed is often sold in sheets but can also be found in flakes, making it a versatile ingredient to have in the pantry. The seaweed flakes are excellent for sprinkling over dishes with beans, vegetables or grains, adding taste as well as nutrients.

Preparation time **10 minutes**
Cooking time **25 minutes**
Level **easy**
Wine **Bolgheri Bianco**

rice noodles in shiitake broth

Ingredients for 4 servings

Noodles:

2 dried shiitake mushrooms

2 tbsps sesame oil

1 white onion, thinly sliced

2 carrots, peeled and diced

1 celery heart, thinly sliced

4 cups (1 litre) hot water

1 tbsp rice miso

4-5 chives, minced

7 oz (200 g) very thin rice noodles

Soak the dried mushrooms in water for 10 minutes, then drain, squeeze out and thinly slice.

Heat the sesame oil in a saucepan and sauté the onion until soft. Add the carrots and celery.

Cover with the hot water and add the mushrooms.

Cook for 25 minutes, then stir in the miso and let simmer for 2 minutes. Add the minced chives.

Divide the rice noodles between 4 serving bowls and pour over the boiling soup.

Cover each bowl with a plate and let sit for 7 minutes, then serve immediately, before the noodles overcook.

Soups

2

Shiitake mushrooms, often used in Japanese cuisine, are originally Chinese. They can be found fresh or dried, and are used in soups and mixed vegetable dishes.

Preparation time **10 minutes**
Cooking time **30 minutes**
Level **easy**
Wine **Cirò Bianco**

tortellini in broth

Ingredients for 6 servings

Pasta dough:

3 cups plus 3 tbsps (14 oz or 400 g) all-purpose flour

4 eggs

Filling:

3½ oz (100 g) mortadella, chopped

3½ oz (100 g) prosciutto, chopped

3½ oz (100 g) pork loin, chopped

1¼ cups (4 oz or 140 g) grated Parmesan cheese, plus extra for garnish

1 egg, salt, nutmeg

Broth:

8 cups (2 l) chicken or capon broth

According to Emilian tradition, a small glass of good red wine is added to the soup bowl with the tortellini.

Mix the flour and eggs together to make a smooth dough and form it into a ball. Wrap in plastic wrap and refrigerate for 30 minutes.

Mince the mortadella, prosciutto and pork in a food processor until thoroughly combined. Stir in the Parmesan, egg, a pinch of salt and a grating of nutmeg. Roll the dough out thinly and use a rolling cutter to cut out large squares of dough. Cut the squares into strips and then place spoonfuls of the filling 1 inch (2½ cm) apart along the strips. Cut the dough into squares with the filling in the center of each square, then fold over from opposite corners to make a triangle. Press down well around the edges, then wrap each triangle around the little finger, giving it a half twist, and press the opposing corners together to make the tortellini. Let them sit out on a tray to dry. Bring the broth to a boil and cook the tortellini. Just before they are done, remove from the heat and let them finish cooking off the heat. Serve them in shallow soup bowls, sprinkled with Parmesan.

Preparation time **30 minutes**
Cooking time **8 minutes**
Level **medium**
Wine **Sangiovese dei Colli Bolognesi**

chickpea and leek soup
with fresh pappardelle

Ingredients for 4 servings
Pasta dough:

3 eggs, salt, **2½** cups (11½ oz or 320 g)
all-purpose flour

Soup:

3/4 cup (5½ oz or 150 g) dried
chickpeas, soaked overnight

3 garlic cloves, unpeeled

1 carrot, minced, **3-4** sage leaves

3 tbsps extra-virgin olive oil

1 white onion, finely minced

1 celery stalk, minced

4 cups (1 litre) light vegetable broth

salt and pepper, **2** ripe tomatoes

Garnish:

rosemary, minced (optional)

Mix the flour, eggs and salt together to form a smooth dough. Wrap in plastic wrap and refrigerate.
Cook the soaked chickpeas in a pressure cooker with water, the garlic and sage leaves for 40 minutes. Drain, reserving the cooking liquid. Discard the garlic and sage.
Heat the olive oil in a saucepan and sauté the onion.
Add the carrot and celery and cook until soft.
Add the chickpeas and cover with hot vegetable broth and some of the chickpea cooking liquid. Season with salt and pepper and let simmer for 10 minutes.
Blanch the tomatoes, peel them and deseed.
Dice the flesh.
Roll the pasta dough out thinly and cut into long, thick strips. Bring a large pot of salted water to a boil and cook the pappardelle.
Drain and add to the soup together with the tomatoes.
Serve hot. Sprinkle with minced rosemary if desired.

Soups

Fresh chickpeas ripen between June and October, but they almost exclusively sold dried or canned. When buying dried chickpeas make sure they are no more than a year and a half old and that they have no cracks or holes in them.

Preparation time **30 minutes**
Cooking time **50 minutes**
Level **medium**
Wine **Bardolino Chiaretto**

rice vermicelli
with chicken and vegetables

Ingredients for 4 servings
Soup:

5½ oz (150 g) chicken breast

2 tbsps extra-virgin olive oil

1 shallot, thinly sliced

1 small mild red chili pepper, minced

salt

1 carrot, peeled and julienned

1 small zucchini, julienned

1 celery stalk, fibers removed, julienned

3½ oz (100 g) rice vermicelli

fresh ginger, grated

parsley, minced

Slice the chicken breast in small pieces, then set aside.
Heat the olive oil in a saucepan and sauté the shallot
and chili until soft. Add the chicken, season with salt,
and cook gently for 2 minutes.
Add the carrot, zucchini and celery and cover with hot
water. Let cook for about 3 minutes over low heat,
then add the rice vermicelli.
Cook for another 6-7 minutes, then add a pinch of freshly
grated ginger and adjust the salt.
Add the parsley and serve.

Preparation time **15 minutes**
Cooking time **25 minutes**
Level **easy**
Wine **Trentino Müller Thurgau**

basic techniques

Pasta

BASIC DOUGHS

Here are some of the most-used doughs when making fresh pastas.

Garganelli

Ingredients for 4 servings

2⅓ cups plus 1 tbsp (10½ oz or 300 g) all-purpose flour; **1** egg plus **3** egg yolks

Method

Mound the flour on a work surface and make a well in the center. Add the egg and egg yolks in the middle and mix with a fork.

Knead the dough until smooth and free of lumps. Form into a ball, wrap in plastic wrap and refrigerate for 30 minutes. Roll the dough out with a rolling pin into a not-too-thin sheet and cut it into squares about 3 inches (7 cm) on each side.

Roll the squares around a smooth wooden stick, starting from one of the corners and continuing to the diagonally opposite corner.

Roll the curl over a garganelli-making tool, a ridged board (see photo on the right), pressing down lightly.

Remove from the stick and transfer to a floured tray or wooden board.

Orecchiette

Ingredients for 4 servings

2⅓ cups (14 oz or 400 g) semolina flour; salt

Method

Mix the semolina flour with warm water and a pinch of salt to form a firm dough. Form into a ball and cover with a kitchen towel. Break off a small piece of dough and form into a rope about 1/2 inch (1 cm) thick. Cut the rope into many of small pieces. Take each piece and press it down with the thumb or the

another idea

Garganelli pair well with a sauce of shallots, diced ham and fresh peas. Alternatively replace the ham with pancetta for even more flavor.

382

tip of a table knife on a wooden board. Turn the piece inside-out over the tip of the thumb, pressing down lightly to give it an ear shape.

Lasagna Sheets
Ingredients for 4 servings
2⅓ cups plus 1 tbsp (10½ oz or 300 g) all-purpose flour; **3** eggs; salt; **1** tbsp extra-virgin olive oil

Method
Mix the flour and eggs together to form a dough. Shape into a ball, wrap in plastic wrap and refrigerate for 30 minutes.
Roll out the dough into thin sheets and cut them into rectangles 2 by 4 inches (5 by 10 cm).
Bring a large pot of salted water to a boil and add the olive oil. Cook the lasagna sheets for a few minutes, then carefully drain them with a slotted spoon and lay on a clean kitchen towel to dry.

Tagliatelle
Ingredients for 4 servings
2⅓ cups plus 1 tbsp (10½ oz or 300 g) all-purpose flour; **3** eggs

Method
Mix together the flour and eggs and knead well to form a smooth dough.
Wrap in plastic wrap and refrigerate for 30 minutes.
Roll out with a rolling pin or pasta machine to form very thin sheets. Flour the sheets and roll them up, then slice them into tagliatelle with a sharp knife. Alternatively, use the pasta machine's tagliatelle attachment to cut the sheets. Flour the tagliatelle and arrange on a clean kitchen towel to dry before cooking in abundant salted boiling water.

advice
Remember that tagliatelle and all egg pastas should be cooked only to the al dente stage, retaining a bit of bite.

Basic Techniques

383

Filled Pasta

Fresh pastas filled with different ingredients offer huge scope for creativity and imagination.

Making good agnolotti or ravioli requires skill, good taste and experience. Pairing shapes and fillings, creating new combinations and working pasta so that it keeps the right consistency during cooking are all difficult tasks, but when done right they produce impressive results.

Tortelloni

Ingredients for 4 servings

2 cups (9 oz or 250 g) all-purpose flour; **1** egg plus **3** egg yolks; salt

Method

Mound the flour on a work surface and make a well in the center. Add the egg and egg yolks and a pinch of salt in the middle and work the dough until smooth and free of lumps. Form into a ball, wrap in plastic wrap and refrigerate for 30 minutes. Roll the dough out thinly on a floured wooden pastry board.

Along half the dough place little piles of the filling, about an inch (2-3 cm) apart. Fold over the other half of the dough and press around the filling with the fingertips. Cut out squares with a rolling fluted cutter to form tortelloni.

Tortellini

Ingredients for 4 servings

2¾ cups (12½ oz or 350 g) all-purpose flour; 3 eggs

Method

Mound the flour on a work surface and make a hollow in the center. Break the eggs into the middle and work the dough until smooth and free of lumps.

advice
Fresh pasta can be stored in the refrigerator for up to 24 hours, or frozen for up to 3 months. However best results will be obtained if it is cooked as soon as it is made.

Form into a ball, wrap in a clean kitchen towel and refrigerate for 30 minutes. Roll the pasta out on a wooden pastry board and make it as thin as possible. Cut out squares of about 1 inch (2½ cm) each side.

Place a small quantity of filling in the middle of each square. Fold into a triangle, from opposite corner to opposite corner. Place the triangle on the index finger, then press the two points together, pressing well to seal (see photo on the left). This characteristic ring shape is said to be an imitation of Venus's navel.

Anolini

Ingredients for 4 servings
2⅓ cups plus 1 tbsp (10½ oz or 300 g) all-purpose flour; **3** eggs

Method
Mound the flour on a work surface and make a well in the center. Break the eggs into the middle and work the dough until smooth. Form into a ball, wrap in plastic wrap and refrigerate for 30 minutes.

Roll the dough out into a thin sheet. Cut into wide strips and dot the strips with small quantities of filling. Then either fold the strip over itself, if wide enough, or close by placing another strip of dough on top.

Press around the filling, then cut them into small serrated rectangles with a cookie cutter or anolini cutter.

The proper filling for anolini, as well as the broth they are cooked in, is a hotly debated subject. Anolini are one of the oldest traditional stuffed pastas.

The filling is always based on beef or donkey meat, cooked for a very long time -between 16 and 36 hours. However around Piacenza a variant is based on egg, nutmeg and very aged Parmesan cheese.

Cappelletti, in Emilia and Romagana, are very similar to tortellini. However they should have a slimmer and more graceful form. Tortellini contain less filling and are made with a thinner dough.

basic rules

For pasta which is bright yellow with a dense consistency, use the same amount of flour indicated in the recipe, but use only 6-8 egg yolks instead of whole eggs. This dough can be kneaded for longer, and should be worked vigorously.

Basic Techniques

385

BASIC SAUCES

Here are some recipes for tomato-based sauces, with some flavorful variations, and a basic pesto recipe. Tomatoes, on their own or with other ingredients, are without doubt the most common and popular sauce for every shape of pasta.

It is hard to imagine today that for over 500 years pasta was consumed without this simple and tasty sauce.

The first use of the tomato as food in Italy seems to have been in Naples. Towards the end of the 18th century its good conservation qualities were discovered, and soon after the tomato began to appear in cookbooks, marking its official entry into the Italian diet.

Since then it has become fundamental, from north to south.

Classic Tomato Sauce

Ingredients for 4 servings

2-3 tbsps extra-virgin olive oil; **1/2** carrot, peeled and minced; **1** celery stalk, fibers removed, minced; **1/2** white onion, minced; **1** cup (7 oz or 200 g) canned, peeled plum tomatoes, in their juice; **5** basil leaves; salt

Method

Heat the olive oil in a saucepan and sauté the carrot, celery and onion for 3-4 minutes over low heat. Either crush the tomatoes with a spoon or pass them through a food mill, then add to the pan and cook gently for around 10 minutes, stirring often. Add the basil leaves and a pinch of salt at the end.

Another idea

The peeled tomatoes can also be replaced by canned, crushed tomatoes. The carrot, celery and onion can be minced in a food processor, but pulse it so as not to overheat the vegetables.

a secret
Adding a pinch of sugar to the tomatoes during cooking helps soften their acidity.

Spicy Tomato Sauce

Ingredients for 4 servings

1 garlic clove; **1/2** red chili pepper (dried or fresh); **3** tbsps extra-virgin olive oil; **1** cup (6½ oz or 180 g) canned, crushed tomatoes; salt and pepper

Method

Peel the garlic clove and cut it in half. Discard the inner green shoot and mince the rest. Deseed the chile and either crumble it or finely mince it.

Heat the olive oil in a saucepan with the garlic and chile. Just before the garlic colors add the tomatoes and cook over medium heat for 10 minutes, adding a little water halfway through and seasoning with pinches of salt and pepper to taste.

Another idea

The amount of garlic and chile can be varied according to taste. However the chili seeds should always be removed as they are strong and not very aromatic. If you don't like too much garlic, leave the clove whole and lightly smash it, then brown briefly in the oil and remove before adding the tomatoes. In the summer the crushed tomatoes can be replaced by fresh, ripe tomatoes, blanched, peeled, deseeded and chopped.

Amatriciana Variation

Brown a thinly sliced white onion in a frying pan with 3 tablespoons extra-virgin olive oil, then add about 3½ oz (100 g) pancetta cut into matchsticks.

As soon as the fat starts to render add 1 cup (6½ oz or 180 g) canned, crushed tomatoes and cook for around 10 minutes. Season generously with salt and pepper. The original recipe from the town of Amatrice involves pasta tossed with guanciale (cured pig jowl) browned in oil, then sprinkled with pepper and grated Pecorino Romano cheese.

advice

The choice between a sweeter or spicier sauce is a question of taste. However if you like strong flavors, make sure not to use too much sauce with the pasta, or risk completely masking the basic flavor of the pasta.

Mediterranean Variation

Blanch 3 ripe San Marzano (or plum) tomatoes for 30 seconds, then immerse in cold water. Peel, deseed and chop.

Sauté 1 smashed garlic clove (or 1/2 minced clove) in 3 tablespoons extra-virgin olive oil with 2 teaspoons pine nuts and 2 anchovy fillets in oil.

Add 1 cup (6½ oz or 180 g) canned, crushed tomatoes, 5 desalted capers and 15 olives. Continue cooking with a little of the pasta cooking water. Stir in basil and salt and pepper to taste.

Spiced Vegetable Variation

Sauté 1 minced spring onion in a frying pan with 3 tablespoons extra-virgin olive oil. Add 1/2 diced red bell pepper and sauté for 5 minutes.

Deseed and dice 1/2 eggplant and 2 zucchini and add to the pan with 3/4 cup (3½ oz or 100 g) peas. Separately heat 3/4 cup (5½ oz or 150 g) canned crushed tomatoes, then add to the vegetables with 1 teaspoon mixed ground spices (cumin, nutmeg, coriander).

Cook for around 10 minutes. Adjust salt and pepper.

Alla Norma Variation

Thinly slice 1 eggplant, sprinkle with salt and leave in a colander for at least 30 minutes.

Sauté 1 smashed garlic clove in a frying pan with 2 tablespoons extra-virgin olive oil. Add 3 chopped tomatoes to the pan. Cook for 2 minutes then add basil. Remove from the heat and set aside. Rinse the eggplant, pat dry and chop.

Fry in hot sunflower oil. Drain on paper towels, then add to the tomatoes together with cooked pasta (spaghetti or penne).

Sprinkle with 2 tablespoons grated ricotta salata and stir just before serving.

a secret
To ease peeling, cut an X in the base of the tomatoes before blanching.

Pesto

Pesto is another historic sauce, originally from Liguria, though there exist infinite variations. The official recipe dates back to the 19th century, but draws on much older traditions.

Genoan Pesto

Ingredients for 6 servings
35-40 leaves Ligurian basil; coarse salt; **4-5** garlic cloves; **2** tbsps grated Pecorino Sardo; **2** tbsps grated Parmesan cheese; **6** tbsps extra-virgin olive oil

Method
Crush the basil, salt and garlic with a mortar and pestle until mashed. Add the grated cheeses and continue to work the mixture with a wooden spatula, scraping it off the sides.
When the paste is smooth add the oil, pouring in a thin stream and stirring to obtain a smooth cream.

advice
It's best to use a wooden or stone mortar, because metal can alter the flavor of the basil. With a food processor, pulse it so the basil doesn't heat up and discolor.

basic tools

Pasta

1 Ravioli mold An old-fashioned ravioli mold makes forming filled pastas much easier. A sheet of dough is placed over the mold, filling placed in the little hollows, then another sheet of pasta laid across and rolled over with a rolling pin to cut out the individual ravioli.

2 Pasta pot A pot with a built-in strainer, so pasta can be cooked and drained with ease. Can also be used for boiling asparagus and steaming vegetables.

3 Bronze stamp for cappelletti and ravioli Classic utensils with large, comfortable grips, round or square for cutting out filled pasta. The internal spring helps close the pasta while expelling any trapped air.

4 Spring-loaded tongs With long, ridged grips to help grasp spaghetti when serving.

5 Cookie cutters Very useful to have in a range of sizes and shapes (round, square, triangular; fluted, serrated, smooth) for cutting out fresh pasta.

6 Spaghetti Measure With holes indicating one or two portions of spaghetti, plus a little hook at the end to capture a single piece of spaghetti to test for doneness.

7 Plastic cappelletti mold A classic shape in a modern material, pairing innovation and tradition.

8 Large Spider Skimmer Bigger than a normal skimmer, it has many uses, such as quickly scooping out cooked short pasta while leaving the water in the pot, to be used again. Can also be used for potatoes and other boiled vegetables.

9 Double rolling cutter in brass For cutting sheets of dough with serrated edges.

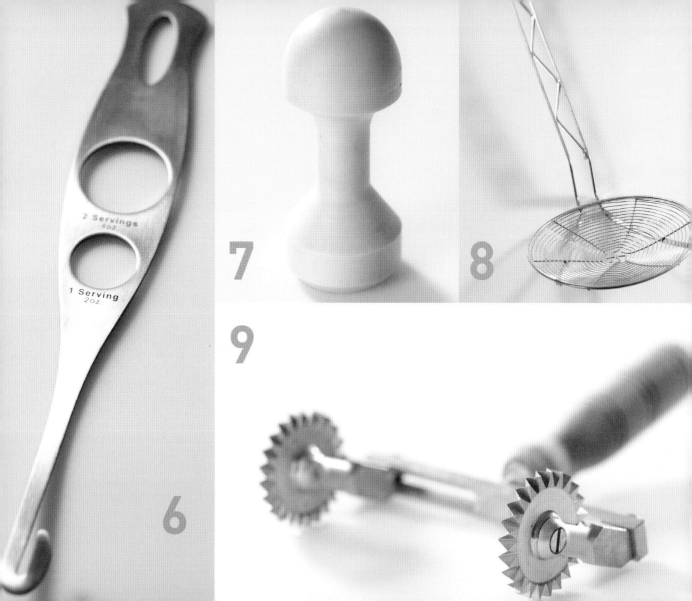

6

2 Servings
4oz.

1 Serving
2oz.

7

8

9

index

Pasta

Pasta

index

397

Pasta & Co.

Published in 2008 by
Leonardo Publishing srl
Via Bordoni, 8 - 20124
MILAN - Italy
www.leonardopublishing.com

Published originally under the title "Pasta & Co."
© 2005 Food Editore srl
Via Mazzini, 6 - 43100 PARMA
www.foodeditore.com

English Translation
Traduzioni Culinarie

Photographs
Alberto Rossi and Davide Di Prato

Recipes
Simone Rugiati and Licia Cagnoni

Printed in China in 2008